1830-2005

Steam Packet 175

the official
anniversary book of
the
Isle of Man
Steam Packet Company

compiled by
Miles Cowsill
and **John Hendy**

contributors
Stan Basnett, Peter Corrin,
Jack Ronan, John Shepherd

STEAM PACKET COMPANY
175th ANNIVERSARY

Ferry Publications
PO Box 33,
Ramsey,
Isle of Man IM99 4LP

Tel: +44 (0) 1624 898445
Fax: +44 (0) 1624 898449

E-mail: FerryPubs@aol.com

Website: www.ferrypubs.co.uk

FERRY
Publications

*The **SeaCat Danmark** gets underway for Belfast. in June 1998. The famous Tower of Refuge lies beyond in Douglas Bay.* (Miles Cowsill)

Acknowledgements

The publishers are grateful for the support of both Hamish Ross, Managing Director of the Isle of Man Steam Packet Company and Juan Kelly, the Chairman of the Company for their encouragement and support with the production of this publication. The Public Relations Manager of the Isle of Man Steam Packet Company, Geoff Corkish, is also thanked for all his hours of support and assistance. The contribution by Captain Peter Corrin, the Marine Superintendent to this title is also very much appreciated. Our thanks also go to Captain Jack Ronan, Stan Basnett and John Shepherd, who have assisted with this publication with many hours of research and checking of proofs.

The publishers are grateful to the following also for their assistance:

John Clarkson, Bruce Peter, Stephen Harrison and Roger Sims of Manx National Heritage, Emma Challinor, Wirral Archives, Glasgow University Archives, the Imperial War Museum, Island Photographic, Phil Thomas, E.D. Lace, Ray Smith, Liverpool Maritime Museum, Andrew Lowe, Ian Collard, Dick Clague, Ian Smith, David and Dorothy Parsons, Jeffrey Sankey and Andrew Barton.

As usual, a word of thanks to the Ferry Publications staff: Pat Somner, Clare Price and Timothy Cowsill for their involvement with the project.

Published by Ferry Publications Ltd
PO Box 33, Ramsey, Isle of Man,
British Isles, IM99 4LP
Tel: +44 (0) 1624 898445 Fax: +44 (0) 1624 898449
E Mail: ferrypubs@aol.com

Contents

*The **Lady of Mann** (2) makes ready for departure from Douglas in January 2005 for the afternoon sailing to Liverpool.* (Miles Cowsill)

175

Introduction

Any important anniversary is worth celebrating and the year 2005 marks the 175th anniversary of the foundation of the Isle of Man Steam Packet Company.

This event in itself is something rather special and of which the Manx nation can feel justly proud. However, this remarkable episode should not simply be seen in the context of a noble island in the middle of the Irish Sea but must also be recognised in the annals of world shipping. The reason for this is simple for although the Steam Packet was certainly not the first shipping company to be founded, it is today the oldest existing such concern on the planet. Such events should certainly be the cause for much commemoration and praise. This eulogy therefore seeks to honour the distinguished Company which is the subject of our present book. The illustrious life and times of the Steam Packet Company have included occasions which have been joyful, solemn and also innovative.

But the 175 years is not just the story of the ships which have so reliably provided the vital Manx lifeline with the rest of the British Isles and enabled the Island to grow and prosper. Neither is it simply the story of the routes on which the ships have plied linking the Island at one time or another with England, Wales, Scotland, Ulster and the Republic of Ireland. It is also the story of the Manx people who have worked for the Steam Packet throughout its 175 years. As we shall see in Captain Ronan's chapter concerning the Masters, the vast majority of them came from very humble seafaring backgrounds and learned their craft in the fishing fleets of Castletown, Peel, Port St Mary and Port Erin. Joining the Steam Packet fleet on the lowest rung of the ladder, through their own hard work and determination they were able to rise through the ranks to achieve the highest honours which gained them tremendous respect from their fellow countrymen. To be a Steam Packet Captain was certainly the pinnacle of any Manxman's career at sea. Some were to go even further and took on important managerial roles ashore.

This simple pattern of promotion had its foundations firmly anchored the earliest days of the Steam Packet and would have certainly been recognised in Nelson's Navy at the Battle of Trafalgar, some 25 years before the foundation of the Isle of Man Company. Within island communities things are slow to change and that is perhaps one of their endearing qualities and strengths.

The rail and tramway transport networks of the Isle of Man are Victorian in both their modes of locomotion and in their

Miles Cowsill and John Hendy. (Richard Seville)

infrastructure. When John Hendy first visited the Isle of Man in 1982, each of the four car ferries and the passenger steamer *Manxman* was operated with just one crew and even during the middle of the summer, each unit would lay-by for one day each week while the crew rested. The fleet and the method of its operation presented a sharp contrast to working practices found elsewhere around the coast. Things happened simply because they had always been like that and on the principal link between Douglas and Liverpool, two ships were operated on the winter service for a single daily trip, returning the following day.

However, the nature of the ferry industry continued to change and unwanted competition linked with a sharp downturn in summer tourists forced the Company to face new, and to some unwelcome, challenges.

The end of steam-powered ships with that oh so familiar blast from their distinctive triple-chime whistles prior to leaving their berths on the Victoria and Edward Piers was certainly the end of an era. The end of the daily cargo service to Liverpool and the introduction of roll on - roll off ferries opened a new chapter in the Island's history as did the switch of mainland port from historic Liverpool, with its broad and famous river forever linked with the Steam Packet, to the quieter and enclosed haven at Heysham.

With Sea Containers pioneering the introduction of high-speed catamarans on UK - Continental routes, this period of the Company's history also saw the introduction of fast ferries on Manx services which brought new opportunities to the existing trades, particularly for day-trippers embarking for Liverpool on shopping sprees or sporting fixtures.

The loss of the Steam Packet's independence when it was taken over by Bermuda-based Sea Containers in 1996 could have been the end of the story but although the familiar livery was changed, the name remained and the Company continued to ply its trade on the well-worn sea routes of the Irish Sea.

The entry into service of an entirely new type of ferry, the Dutch-built ro-pax *Ben-my-Chree*, came about in 1998. Gone were the familiar lines and looks which had for so long been the hallmark of the Company as the ship with the totally new profile made her way into Douglas Harbour for the first time. Although she may lack the flair and sheer of the earlier ships, the 'Ben' combines her dual roles of freight and passenger/ car ferry with a day in - day out reliability which even twenty years ago the Masters of the Steam Packet would have found quite alien.

In 2003 the Steam Packet was again sold, this time to UK company Montagu Private Equity Ltd., and the much-loved Steam Packet funnel was reinstated.

Even the 175th anniversary of the Company will be tinged with a degree of sadness as the very last, traditional Isle of Man Steam Packet Company side-loading car ferry *Lady of Mann* will be retired after 29 loyal years of service during which time she has kept the precious lifeline open in all weathers, no matter what the Irish Sea has chosen to throw at her.

Ever sensitive to its maritime traditions, the Company will see the 'Lady' out in style and an imaginative programme of special sailings has been arranged to Llandudno, Liverpool, Fleetwood,

*The Shelter Deck on board the **Mona's Queen** (3). (Ferry Publications Library)*

Whitehaven and Troon - the place of her birth.

The Steam Packet is also arranging other special events to mark a remarkable milestone in its history. It is to be hoped that both Islanders and the Company's many devotees will wish to join these historic celebrations and show their own appreciation of the Steam Packet's magnificent service to the Isle of Man.

Miles Cowsill,
Ramsey,
Isle of Man

John Hendy
Ivychurch,
Kent

*The double-ended **Mona** (3) makes an impressive view leaving the port of Ramsey with a full load of passengers. (Stan Basnett collection)*

Preface

This celebratory book is a history of the Steam Packet, a Manx company, of its people and their role during its 175 years as the institutional lifeline of the Isle of Man.

It is a story of bold initiatives, intense competition, financial disasters narrowly averted, changing ownership, dramatic reductions in passenger numbers, and wartime courage. The political and economic background has been a thriving British Empire, the major world depression of the 1930's, two World Wars and the advent of affordable international travel, to list only some of the external influences during the lifetime of the Company.

The Steam Packet was founded and began to operate its first ship in 1830, that is before the Boer War, before the future Queen Victoria came to the throne, before Isambard Kingdom Brunel built his first iron ship. This bold local initiative was at the instigation of Manx residents, weary of stormy and frequently unsuccessful attempts to cross the Irish Sea in ships hardly worthy of the name. Hence the *Mona's Isle*, the first of the 71 ships owned by the Steam Packet, arrived to great popular acclaim in August 1830.

Since that enterprising start, the Steam Packet has not been without excitement. Ownership varied from private to public, listed on the London Stock Exchange, and back to private again in the hands of Sea Containers, and now Montagu Private Equity. Intense competition threatened Company viability several times; firstly in the very early days of the Steam Packet, then in 1887, and again in 1985 when financial disaster was avoided only by a merger between the Company and its Manx Line competitor.

Between times passenger numbers had grown steadily from the late 1880's, as the availability of a regular ferry service and the introduction of the Tourist Trophy Races in 1907 made the Isle of Man a tourist Mecca. Up to 18 ships catered for well over half a million tourists a year. But post WW2, passenger numbers dropped dramatically, as affordable international travel took tourists further afield. The advent of exciting high speed craft, the result of major improvements in marine design and shipbuilding, has been enthusiastically embraced by the Company as a way to stimulate passenger numbers once again. But, realistically, the much smaller fleet we have today will suffice for the foreseeable future.

No Steam Packet history would be seriously complete without reference to the World Wars, when a total of 21 ships, 8 of which were lost, were involved on active duty. We should not fail to salute the Steam Packet mariners who manned them with exemplary courage, nonetheless real for being now so long past.

Juan Kelly
(IOMSP Co Ltd)

This book is first and foremost a factual account of the Steam Packet over the last 175 years. It is also a tribute to all those past and present who have striven keenly for the good of the Company and those it serves. Pride in this past gives real encouragement to us all to make sure that the Steam Packet of the future is one of which the Island community, customers and staff can more than ever be justifiably proud.

Juan Kelly, Chairman
April 2005

Foreword

Hamish Ross. (IOMSP Co Ltd)

Publication of this fine book marks a very special year in the long history of the Isle of Man Steam Packet Company.

Founded in 1830 the Company has a proud record of service to the Island and indeed through two World Wars to the British Nation as a whole. Despite its age the Steam Packet is a modern progressive company, proud of its past, but determined to provide excellent service to the Island now and in the future. Our mix today of fast and conventional ferries allows us to provide a frequency and reliability of service to properly serve the demands of both the freight and passenger sectors of our business.

This well-written and researched book with a rich variety of photographs of ships and people will be a fascinating read for anyone whose life has in any way been touched by the Steam Packet. Above all it will stand as a fitting tribute to the ships and the women and men afloat and ashore who have served the Company since its formation and to their achievements.

As we enter our 175th year all of us at the Steam Packet feel privileged to be playing a part in the ongoing story of a very special shipping company.

We at the Steam Packet are proud of the Island we serve and we hope that many people on the Island are equally proud of the historic shipping company which has over many years provided their 'lifeline' services.

Hamish Ross, Managing Director
April 2005

An outstanding view of the *Fenella* (2) being launched at Vickers Armstrong, Barrow on 16th December 1936. (Jeffrey D Sankey)

CHAPTER ONE

The Mail Contract

by Stan Basnett

In 1767 the British Government passed an Act authorising their Post Office to conduct mail to and from the Isle of Man, to establish post offices and post roads as necessary and to establish a packet boat between the port of Whitehaven (Cumberland) and Douglas.

Prior to 1767 the Isle of Man was not within the remit of the Post Office and the conveyance of mail to and from the Island was at best erratic and not secure even for official communications, although for seventeen years prior to the Act a privately-owned packet boat had operated a service between Whitehaven and Douglas.

Under the new Act, Douglas was made a sub-office of Whitehaven and the mail contract was awarded to a Whitehaven syndicate to provide a weekly return sailing, weather permitting, for a fee of £150 per annum. The sailings were very much dependent on the vagaries of the weather - in 1813 the mail packet actually completed fifty two round voyages, yet in December 1821 only one round voyage was possible in six weeks owing to persistent gales. Given fair weather the passage took about six hours and the fare was 10/6d (52.5p). Adverse weather was still to cause delays to the post and smuggling, so long a way of life around the ports of the Irish Sea, was often more profitable than the mail!

Until 1819, communication between the Isle of Man and the rest of the British Isles remained the domain of sailing vessels most of which were traders. The *Duke of Athol* and *Lapwing* however also carried mail and passengers. The port of despatch for the mail was Whitehaven which, being exposed to westerly gales, caused many delays.

Dissatisfaction with the service continued with local merchants and officials taking matters into their own hands and passing letters to masters of vessels and passengers bound for Liverpool for onward transmission on arrival. Not only was the Governor amongst those complaining but also the Bishop and the commanding officer of the garrison at Castle Rushen.

Steamer Services

The advent of steamer services on the Irish Sea and elsewhere by the second decade of the nineteenth century saw the Whitehaven contractors and the Post Office under more threat to improve their service. The Whitehaven contractors acquired a bigger sailing vessel and undertook to provide eighty sailings a year. Adverse weather and competition conspired against them so

much that the islanders, to the annoyance of the Post Office, continued to use the steamers and the port of Liverpool as their preferred option.

The first mention of a steamer in Manx waters was at the end of June 1815 when the *Henry Bell* anchored in Ramsey Bay. The 30-ton *Triton* provided the first regular winter service in 1825, sailing once a week between Whitehaven and Douglas. The first attempt to form a Manx company to operate a steamer service was made in 1826 when Mark Cosnahan, a Manxman living in Liverpool, purchased the new steamer *Victory* and offered shares in her at £50 each. Sadly for the Island, the project came to nothing.

With steam packet vessels such as the *Enterprise* (under the command of Capt. Robert Crawford) maintaining a weekly return service between Liverpool, Ramsey and Greenock and the *St Andrew* sailing between Whitehaven, Douglas and Dublin in addition to numerous individual steam-driven general traders running between Liverpool and Douglas, it was not surprising that merchants and Government officials preferred to use the steamers, using agents or masters of the vessels to forward their mail on arrival in Liverpool. This frequently saved days on delivery.

The result was inevitable and the Post Office were forced to change the port of despatch to Liverpool in 1822 and at the same time Douglas was upgraded to become a Crown Office. The lucrative Liverpool - Isle of Man mail contract was won by the locally-owned St George Steam Packet Co.. They undertook to provide the service for an annual sum of £300 per annum employing different steamers as available and at best rates obtainable. However, the service was still not to the satisfaction of the Manx public.

The 'Manx Advertiser' and the 'Manx Sun' advertised the order of sailings of His Majesty's Royal Mail Packet *St David* for passengers only between Liverpool and Douglas with three return sailings per week boarding without the aid of small boats. Departures from Liverpool were from George's Pierhead and The Quay in Douglas. The Liverpool agents were John Watson of 21 Water Street and the Douglas agent was David Forbes of New Bond Street.

But as with all contractors before, the mail contract was seen as a guaranteed income with the provision of a service as a secondary consideration. As a consequence, several unsuccessful attempts were made to form a Manx shipping company to bring control under the Island and guarantee a reliable service.

The Isle of Man Steam Packet Co. Ltd. Board of Directors 1903
E. J Baldwin, A. W. Moore, D. Maitland, J. T. Cowell, T. Stuttard
W. A. Waid, J. J. Goldsmith

The Isle of Man Steam Packet Co. Ltd. Board of Directors 1910

R. T. Curphey, W. A. Waid, C.T.W. Hughes-Games, W. H. Kitto, D. Maitland, E. J. Baldwin, J. G. Elliott (Chairman)

The Isle of Man Steam Packet Co. Ltd. Board of Directors 1930
Left to Right: W.H.Kitto, G.Fred Clucas, W.H.Dodd, C.T.W. Hughes-Games (Chairman), J.B.Waddington, E.Gordon Thin, A.H. Teare and
W.G. Barwell (General Manager)

The St George Co. placed their older vessels on the route leaving their flagship on the Irish station plying to Dublin. Enough was enough, now there really was a groundswell of public opinion expressing concern that the conduct of mail between the Island and England ought to be under the control of the Island. The only way that this could be achieved was for the Island to have its own steamship company.

Foundation

A meeting was duly called and the minute book from that meeting interestingly enough is titled "Minute book containing the transactions of the Isle of Man Steam Packet Company". The first entry is dated 17th December 1829 and records :–

"Meeting held at Dixon and Steel's saleroom of several inhabitants of Douglas this day for the purpose of establishing a steam packet company, the following resolutions were agreed to:

"The High Bailiff James Quirk was in the chair and a committee of fourteen was appointed to progress the resolutions of the meeting, principal amongst which was to obtain the cost of a suitable steam boat. A sum of £4,500 was subscribed at the meeting which was a considerable sum and indicative of the stature of those present. The committee was immediately set the task of raising the capital to £6,000!

"Matters proceeded quickly and the next meeting held two days later drew up the specification for the vessel with a maximum draft of 8 ft and to be propelled by two 40 hp engines. There was to be

accommodation for one hundred passengers, fifty to be cabin class and fifty in the steerage.

"Minutes of a meeting on the 22nd December record that quotes for a suitable vessel be sought from a number of shipbuilders. A deputation comprising the High Bailiff, Dr Garrett and Mr Geneste was instructed to "wait upon Lord Strathallen to thank him for his kindness to interfere respecting the mail". Such a tantalising snippet indicates that the Company was already keen to secure the mail contract from the St George Co. It also indicates that the promoters of the Company were no lightweights and the deputation was also instructed to furnish the Governor with details of the proceedings.

"The contract for the vessel was placed with John Wood of Glasgow and at a meeting in Douglas on 6th April 1830 two names were put forward for the vessel – Princess Victoria and Mona's Isle – the latter being chosen by a 31 vote majority."

The 'Manx Sun' of 16th June carried this report from the 'Greenock Advertiser':

"….the launch of a superior steam vessel of 200 tons called Mona's Isle of Douglas was launched from the building yard of Mr. John Wood, Port Glasgow. She is to be propelled by two engines of superior power now making by Mr. Robert Napier, Vulcan Foundry, Broomeilaw.

We understand she is owned principally by the Isle of Man and is intended to ply between Douglas and Liverpool with passengers and to

be commanded by Captain Robert Crawford late of the steam packet
Enterprise whose skilful management of that vessel is the best pledge
of the judiciousness of his appointment to the Mona's Isle......"

At the time of the launch the vessel was under the command
of Capt. Crawford but he resigned on 17th July. Two days later
Capt. William Gill, Master of the *Douglas Trader* was appointed
Commander of the *Mona's Isle* on an annual salary of £100. The
vessel arrived at Douglas on 15th August 1830 and after an
inaugural trip to Castletown, Port St Mary and the Calf, she then
entered service on the Liverpool route in direct competition with
the St George Company.

The 'Manx Sun' carried an advert for the trip which seems to
indicate that the vessel was late coming to the Island – were there
some pre-delivery problems which were not recorded?

MONA'S ISLE
Steam Packet

Mona's Isle will sail from Douglas to the Menai Bridge and
Bangor on Thursday 5th August at eleven o'clock returning the
following evening.
Fare for the voyage 20s.
An opportunity is thus afforded to the inhabitants of the Island of
visiting that stupendous and interesting work. As the present trip is
only preparatory to her taking her station between this port and
Liverpool, the same excursion will not likely be repeated this season

The advertisement also announced that 'parcels will be
carefully forwarded.' The agents were Edward Moore of Douglas
and Mark Quayle jun. of 15 Nova Scotia, Liverpool and the

Mona's Isle Steam Packet Office is shown as Pier, Douglas.

The many battles that raged between the two rival companies
are legend and eventually the flagship of the St George Co., the *St
George* was placed on the Liverpool station. It was to be the
undoing of the company; disaster came in the form of a south
easterly gale and the vessel which had remained at anchor in
Douglas Bay dragged her anchor and was wrecked on St Mary's
Isle - or Conister Rock as it is more popularly known today.
Meanwhile Capt. Gill, who was perhaps more aware of the
exposed position of the bay, had taken the *Mona's Isle* to sea to
ride out the storm.

The master and crew of the *St George* were rescued in what
has become one of the most famous rescues in the early years of
the lifeboat service. It was as a direct consequence of this disaster
that the Tower of Refuge was built on the rock now such a
familiar landmark in Douglas Bay. At that time it was well outside
the harbour at Douglas which was still tidal.

A change of name and a contract secured

The loss of the *St George* meant that the Manx company now
had the upper hand but the mail contract remained with the St
George Co., whose vessels were inferior to the *Mona's Isle*. Much
acrimonious correspondence passed between the two companies
and their agents with the Mona's Isle Steam Packet Co repeatedly
asking the St George Co to transfer the mail contract to them.

In March 1831, in desperation, the Company reluctantly wrote
to Sir Francis Peeling, Secretary to the Royal Mail, requesting the
transfer of the mail contract, perhaps realising that they had been
negotiating with the wrong party. Sir Francis did not reply perhaps
indicating that the Post Office was still smarting from their earlier

175

The Isle of Man Steam Packet Co. Ltd. Board of Directors 1947

disputes with the Island and the Steam Packet Company.

Business for the new Company grew steadily so much so that in the same month they resolved to purchase or charter a new vessel. In the event they decided on the latter course and appointed Capt Peter Milligan as its commander at a salary of £84, the ship to be named *Mona*.

The mail contract was eventually transferred later that year to the Mona's Isle Steamship Co. by which name the Company was known although by September 1831 the Company had styled itself as the Isle of Man Steam Packet Co. and all of its assets transferred by February 1832. It was still the same shareholders and Directors – nothing had changed only the name under which the Company operated.

Now with two ships and the mail contract secured, the Company resolved to commence services between Whitehaven and Dublin in addition to the Liverpool route. An outbreak of cholera in Dublin and quarantine restrictions imposed on all vessels plying between Dublin and Liverpool caused the Company to withdraw the Dublin service in April, just one month after it started. The Island did not escape the cholera epidemic and more than 200 people died as a result.

Despite this, the Company continued to expand its business. Now with increased carrying capacity it embarked on excursion traffic, the *Mona's Isle* running an excursion to Menai Bridge and the *Mona* running additional trips to Whitehaven, Kirkcudbright and Garliestown. The Liverpool agent Mark Quayle meanwhile was engaged with the Post Office negotiating a revised contract for the Company, being instructed on 22nd May 1833 to submit a formal tender for the mail contract of £700. After further negotiation, the contract was finalised in July for a twice weekly service for a fee of £850.

On the Island the Post Office had done little to improve the internal distribution of mail to the annoyance of the Bishop and the Garrison commander at Castletown. As a result of continued pressure, the Royal Mail placed contracts with local contractors for additional mail services between Liverpool and Ramsey and Liverpool and Castletown for £100 per annum.

In 1830 the manorial rights of the fourth Duke of Atholl were sold to the Crown and whilst this may not seem to have any significance to the story of the Steam Packet Co. it probably had influenced those who were behind its formation. It certainly was to affect the smuggling trade as the British Treasury were quick to collect the dues and mineral royalties.

For example in February 1833, the *Mona's Isle* was detained by HM Customs necessitating the *Mona* being transferred from the Whitehaven service to convey the mail to Liverpool. The *Mona* was involved later in the year with smuggling spirits from Dublin. As a consequence, stewards were dismissed and a directive issued to Captains to ensure that such practice ceased. It was a problem that was to persist, occupying much of the Directors' time and on occasion, even disrupting the mail service.

The Steam Packet Co. did not have matters all their own way and in 1837 had to deal with a complaint made by former Directors of the company that they were not providing a satisfactory service and that mail was being mishandled. The Company were forced to write a memo to Lord Lichfield, His Majesty's Postmaster General, maintaining that not only were they complying with their contract but exceeding it by providing a daily service for no extra remuneration.

This was supported by another memorandum to the Postmaster General from Governor Ready and signed by forty other dignitaries including the Speaker of the House of Keys, the Deemsters, Customs Officers, the High Bailiff and the Vicar General. Nothing further was heard!

In 1845 the Liverpool agent reported to the Directors that he had been approached by a Post Office Inspector concerning the renewal of the mail contract. At the same time the steamer *Ben my Chree* was to become the mail steamer on the Liverpool run.

On 16th September 1850 the Directors received a letter from the Admiralty strangely still addressed to the Mona's Isle Steam Co.!

"….I am directed by My Lords Commissioners of the Admiralty to acquaint you that from and on the 1st October next the steam vessel conveying the mails under your contract between Liverpool and the Isle of Man is to leave Liverpool at 8am and Douglas at 10am instead of the present hours."

The Directors responded stating that it was not in their interests to change their times due to the convenience of their passengers and the tides at Douglas. The outcome was that the Steam Packet threatened to retreat to the conditions of their contract. Matters rumbled on and even the Governor and the Bishop were complaining about the frequency of the mail.

The Company tabled proposals that they would contract for three mails per week for £1,700 per annum or four mails for £2,500 per annum. The absence of any letter books from the period and scant reference in the minutes leaves a tantalising gap in the continuing battle between the Company, the Admiralty and the Post Office.

The status quo remained until July 1860 when the Directors reported to the half yearly meeting of shareholders that negotiations for a daily mail service had been under consideration by the Postmaster General for sometime – the Directors declining to leave Liverpool at an earlier hour than half past eleven as this would be ruinous to the passenger trade.

How things had changed!

Ramsey and a rival service

In 1861 the ailing Ramsey Steam Packet Co. eventually succumbed and the Isle of Man Steam Packet, anxious to keep the goodwill of Ramsey people, undertook to provide a weekly mail service previously maintained by the Ramsey company's vessel *Manx Fairy*. The contract was passed to the Steam Packet with the approval of the Post Office. The Steam Packet Co. purchased their premises and other quayside assets which guaranteed their presence in Ramsey until services were withdrawn in 1973.

In 1863 the newly appointed Governor Henry Brougham Loch (later Lord Loch and High Commissioner of South Africa), who proved to be a very active influence over events within the Island, saw the need for a guaranteed daily mail service to the Island and took the matter up once again with the Post Office. They promised to re-open negotiations with the Steam Packet Co. who immediately increased their valuation of the contract to £3,000

The Isle of Man Steam Packet Co. Ltd. Board of Directors 1980
W. Gilbey, F. Kissack, K. Rae, S. Shimmin
A. Alexander, Major Brownsdon, K. Cowley

per annum – the Post Office walked away.

From reference to the annual accounts of the Company, it would appear that the mail contract remained at the annual fee of £900 per annum. However, in 1879 Governor Loch was part of a deputation from the Island who went to London to meet with Treasury Officials as a result of which the Postmaster General was authorised to accept an offer from the Isle of Man Steam Packet Company to carry out a mail service between Liverpool and Douglas six days a week throughout the year for the annual sum of £4,500 per annum, nearly four times the existing fee!

The Steam Packet had won but the reason was deeply embedded in unrelated battles with the British Treasury and it was only Governor Loch's determination that saw the way through the entrenched views of both sides. It had taken all his drive and diplomatic skills and now at last the Island had got what it had wanted for so long - a daily despatch of mail to and from the Isle of Man and Liverpool.

It was also during this time that the low water landing pier was built at Douglas. It was suggested to the Governor that the pier be named Loch Pier in his honour but this was declined. In 1872 he unveiled the Victoria Pier alongside which vessels could land at all states of the tide. The implication for the mail was that instead of the risky operation of transferring it at low water by small boat, it

would be discharged directly to the post carts from the steamer.

In 1883, a parcels service was introduced and by 1886 the Company had introduced a midnight steamer from Douglas to Liverpool into their timetable for the conveyance of mail. Two years later, and still trying to find a quicker way of getting mail to London, the Company carried mail to Holyhead to connect with the Irish Mail train.

Although there was a significant improvement in the timing of the inward mail the venture did not prove profitable as Liverpool was the preferred destination for passengers and still more profitable than the mail. To make things more difficult, the Company had to deal with the Isle of Man, Liverpool and Manchester Steam Ship Co. more usually known as the Manx Line which was operating in direct competition on the Liverpool route.

By a strange twist of fate Spencer Walpole, who followed Loch as Lieut. Governor in 1882, became Permanent Secretary to the General Post Office in London after an eleven year term of office. Now there would be no excuse for the Post Office failing to know about the problems of the Isle of Man.

Relations with the Post Office became so cordial that it was not unknown for the departure of the mail packet to be delayed if there had been problems with collections from within the Island. However, as the Steam Packet business continued to expand, it

The Isle of Man Steam Packet Co. Ltd. Board of Directors 2003

John Watt (Planning & Development Manager and not a board member), Walter Gilbey, Robert Quayle, David Benson (Sea Containers), Dursley Stott, Douglas Grant (Finance Manager not board member), Mark Woodward (Chief Operations Manager not board member) Front row seated: Juan Kelly CBE (Chairman), James B Sherwood (President Seaco), Hamish Ross (Managing Director)

became necessary to increase the Liverpool sailings and two departures were introduced. The first was too early for the mail arriving from London and the second too late - once again the conflict of interests raised its head. The Company now suffering the wrath of businesses which were receiving their London mail twenty-four hours late in the summer period!

Unchallenged

The conveyance of mail with the IOM Steam Packet Co. remained unchallenged until 1934 when the advent of air travel became a reality. An airmail service was introduced by the Post Office with a contract awarded to Railway Air Services and 797 letters were carried on the first flight using a DH84 De Havilland Dragon. Other airlines followed and the Post Office was not slow to realise the advantages in time saved and in 1937 the Liverpool mail contract was awarded to Blackpool and West Coast Air Services.

The Steam Packet was left with the parcels traffic but in an effort to keep its interest in the mail contract eventually became part of a syndicate which formed Isle of Man Air Services Ltd and handled the mail contract until taken over by BEA in 1947. Notwithstanding the Company's foray into air traffic, mail was still handled by their vessels which maintained a daily service under the terms of their existing contract.

Despite the advent of regular air services between the Island and the UK, the bulk of the mail throughout the war years and after was carried by the Steam Packet vessels with Royal Mail vans being a familiar sight on the pier awaiting the arrival of the steamer. All the vessels were fitted with locked mail rooms for the conveyance of the mail bags.

The post-war passenger vessels had a mail room located on the Main Deck behind the Third Class bar fitted with a Chubb security lock. A key was held at Liverpool sorting office and another at Douglas. Eventually the mail room was not big enough for all the mail being carried and a slatted wooden locker was built on the same deck against the engine casing for the additional mail bags.

The problem with the air services during the 50's and 60's was that mail was carried on regular passenger aircraft and the capacity was severely limited by both size and weight to something in the order of 30 – 40 bags. Whereas the Steam Packet offered no restriction with the average amount of mail carried being 70 - 80 bags plus parcels. The letters went by van to Regent Street where the sorting office was located at the rear of the General Post Office. A second van took the parcels to a separate sorting facility in Castle Mona Avenue.

Under the terms of the mail contract, which was between Royal Mail and the Steam Packet, the Company undertook to load and unload the mail from the vans to the vessel and convey it between Liverpool and Douglas. Securing the mail in the lockers on board was the responsibility of the senior postman who accompanied the mail and supervised its loading.

Carrying heavy mail bags from the locker up to the Shelter Deck and then up the steps on the pier was no mean feat, particularly at low water. It was not unknown for loose parcels to have to be retrieved by boat hook on the rare occasion! The biggest traffic carried by Royal Mail at this time was boxed kippers outward from Douglas with as many as ten vans taking them to the boat. Such was the amount of summer traffic for this one item that two special vans were brought over from Liverpool by Royal Mail to cope with the collection each season.

With the advent of the first car ferries, dedicated mail rooms were once again incorporated as a direct consequence of high value bags containing money having been lost in the Great Train Robbery, although parcels were carried separately on the Car Deck.

In 1973 the Isle of Man set up its own postal administration, continuing to use Royal Mail as its UK carrier and at the same time undertaking to deliver their mail on the Island. To all intents and purposes there was no real difference with the mail operation and the contract which the Company had remained with Royal Mail.

The Royal Mail pennant was always hoisted at the foremast by the vessel carrying mail on entering port which gave the Mail Packet preference on entering. When both ports were busy with seasonal traffic, it guaranteed berthing preference to the vessel carrying the mail. This practice continued until the merger with Sealink Manx Line in 1985 which coincided with the move away from Liverpool.

Heysham

Mail was now conveyed in containers by road from Liverpool for despatch from Heysham. After 153 years of the conveyance of mail to the Island it had almost come full circle, the mail originally being despatched to the Island from Whitehaven no more than 40 miles from Heysham.

This move away from Liverpool saw the loss to the Company almost entirely of letter mail and dedicated aircraft were introduced to convey letters to and from the Island. Parcels however continued to be carried by sea and were conveyed by road from Liverpool to Heysham and loaded as unaccompanied trailers. On arrival at Douglas they were taken by Steam Packet vehicles to their former cargo warehouse which the Isle of Man Postal Authority had now leased, where they were sorted and delivered.

In 1995 the IOM Postal Authority completed a new Sorting Office at Spring Valley Industrial Estate with modern letter sorting facilities and a purpose built parcel handling section. A new contract between the Royal Mail and the Steam Packet was drawn up to guarantee loading times for purpose built Royal Mail Parcel Force drop trailers carrying general and priority parcels traffic.

The IOMSP Co. continues to carry mixed mail, letters and parcels, daily to and from the Island with collection and deliveries timed to match the sailing schedules, maintaining the long unbroken connection with Royal Mail since 1832.

175

The Isle of Man Steam Packet Co. Ltd. Board of Directors 2004
Back Row standing left to right: Douglas Grant (Finance) Dursley Stott, Mark Woodward (Operations), Gill Gawne (Secretary), John Watt (Strategy & Planning) Stuart Garrett (Human Resources), Robert Quayle. **Seated**: Walter Gilbey, Hamish Ross (MD), Juan Kelly CBE (Chairman), Simon Pooler (Montagu), Peter Longinotti (Montagu)

The magnificent **Ben-my-Chree** (3) on the measured mile prior to entering service in 1908. The 24-knot steamer was tragically a casualty of the Great War. (Jeffrey D. Sankey collection)

CHAPTER TWO

The Early Years 1830 – 1899

by John Shepherd

1789: *French Revolution began with storming of the
Bastille 14th July*

1805: *Battle of Trafalgar, 21st October*

1815 : *Battle of Waterloo, 18th June*

1825: *First railway opened, Stockton to Darlington*

1830: *The* Mona's Isle *first crossed from Douglas to
Liverpool, 16th August*

1837: *Queen Victoria succeeded to the throne*

1840: *Penny postage instituted*

1847: *Visit to IOM of Queen Victoria*

1861: *American Civil War commenced*

1871: *Victoria Pier at Douglas opened for traffic, 1st July*

1876: *Bell invented the telephone*

1894: *Opening of the Manchester Ship Canal,
1st January*

1899: *Boer War began, 10th October*

Following the formation of the Company, a total of £7,250 was subscribed in 290 shares of £25 and the Company's first steamer was launched from the yard of John Wood, Glasgow on 30th June 1830 and named *Mona's Isle*. The new ship inaugurated the Douglas and Liverpool service on 17th August 1830 carrying 15 saloon and 17 steerage passengers. There was fierce competition with the St George Steam Packet Company's *St. George* until that vessel was wrecked on Conister Rock in Douglas Bay in an easterly gale on 20th November 1830.

On 11th July 1831 the Postmaster General awarded the mail contract to the new Isle of Man Steam Packet Company. The mails had to be carried twice weekly in summer and once weekly during the winter for a sum of £1,000 per annum.

In 1832 a second vessel was ordered from John Wood of Glasgow and a small steamer called the *Mona* entered service in July of that year. She was slightly faster than the 'Isle' and usually crossed between Douglas and Liverpool in seven-and-a-half hours.

This wonderful view of Douglas towards the end of the nineteenth century shows the junction of Victoria Street and Loch Promenade at the Jubilee Clock with a cable car from the Do

The third wooden paddle steamer in the fleet, the *Queen of the Isle*, was completed in 1834. A daily sailing (Sundays excepted) operated that summer, leaving Liverpool at 10.00 and Douglas at 08.00.

A rival Manx company styled the Isle of Man and Liverpool Steam Navigation Company ordered a 300-ton steamer from Steele of Greenock in 1835. She was called the *Monarch* and lasted until the new company collapsed in 1837.

The final wooden steamer in the fleet, the *King Orry* [1] was also the only vessel to be built in the Isle of Man at John Winram's yard at Douglas. The hull was launched on 10th February 1842 and the *Mona's Isle* then towed it to Napier's works at Glasgow for the engines to be installed.

The first iron ship in the Steam Packet fleet was launched on 3rd May 1845 from Robert Napier's yard and was named *Ben-my-Chree* [1]. A second iron paddle steamer was launched by Napier on 28th April 1846 and named *Tynwald* [1]. She was nearly double the size of any of her predecessors and was built to cope with the rapidly increasing traffic. The *Tynwald* had the dubious distinction of being the first Steam Packet vessel whose launch was delayed by a strike in the shipbuilding yard.

The Company's pioneer steamer, the *Mona's Isle*, continued to sail throughout the 1840s, although the Directors had advertised her for sale from 1837. She was reboilered by Napier for £500 in 1845. The pioneer vessel was finally sold for demolition in 1851 for the sum of £580.

The Company was experimenting with new routes and in 1842 commenced sailings to Fleetwood. These continued on a spasmodic and intermittent basis over the next 34 years until a regular summer service was established in 1876.

J. & G. Thomson of Govan launched the *Mona's Queen* [1] on 27th November 1852 and the new ship achieved 13.02 knots on

The Imperial Hotel, later to become the headquarters of the Company. (Ferry Publications Library)

trials. In September 1853 the 'Queen' made a special trip to Dublin with Steam Packet shareholders as passengers to enable them to see Queen Victoria on her visit to the Irish capital.

The Isle of Man Steam Packet Company experienced some competition from 1853 until 1861. A local Ramsey company in the north of the Island built the *Manx Fairy* in 1853 and the following year a group of Castletown (in the south) businessmen built the *Ellan Vannin*. The Castletown venture collapsed in 1857 but the *Manx Fairy* remained on the Ramsey station until 1861.

The Prince's Landing Stage at Liverpool was opened on 1st September 1857 and generated an upsurge in passenger traffic. Passengers could now directly board the Douglas-bound steamer without the delays and inconvenience involved in either being rowed out to a vessel anchored in mid-river, or awaiting the tide to leave the enclosed dock system.

...mway at the lower terminus in Victoria Street and three trams from the Douglas Horse Tramway on Loch Promenade. (Manx Museum)

The Company's first vessel was the wooden-hulled paddle steamer **Mona's Isle** (1). She was built at Port Glasgow in 1830 and entered service between Douglas and Liverpool on 16th August that year. (IOMSP Co Ltd collection)

In 1858 Robert Napier took the *King Orry* [1] in part payment of new construction. The sum of £5,000 was allowed against the cost of the new *Douglas* which was launched at Glasgow on 28th May 1858. The *Douglas* achieved a trials speed of 17.25 knots which reputedly made her the fastest steamship built to date, and she reduced the time for the Liverpool and Douglas passage to between four-and-a-half and five hours.

With the outbreak of the American Civil War, the Confederate Government acquired many fast paddle steamers to run the Federal blockade, and in November 1862 the Steam Packet Company sold the *Douglas* for £24,000 to the Confederate agents Fraser, Trenholm & Company. The steamer sailed to Charleston where she was renamed *Margaret & Jessie* but on her tenth run to beat the blockade of the southern ports, she was captured by the

The **Mona** (1) was the Company's second ship and became a Liverpool tug after her retirement in 1841. (Manx Museum)

The **Queen of the Isle** served with the Company for ten years between 1834 and 1844. (Ferry Publications Library)

*The **Mona's Queen** (1) was launched in 1853 remained in the fleet until 1880.* (Manx Museum)

*The **Douglas** (1) had a fascinating history and after being sold in 1862 crossed the Atlantic to eventually become the USS **Gettysburg**. She ended her days as a survey ship in the Mediterranean and is seen cruising off Naples with Mount Vesuvius in the background.* (Ferry Publications Library)

Federal warship *Nansemond* on 5th November 1863. The former Manx steamer was taken to New York and fitted out as a gunboat for the Federal Navy being renamed USS *Gettysburg* in May 1864. She remained with the U.S. Navy as a transport and survey vessel until decommissioned and sold in Genoa in May 1879.

In the mid 1860s, three generally similar paddle steamers were launched for the Steam Packet Company from the yard of Caird &

Company of Greenock. They were the *Snaefell* [1] in 1863 the *Douglas* [2] in 1864 and the *Tynwald* [2] in 1866.

The difficulties of landing and embarking large numbers of passengers at Douglas were overcome in 1871 with the opening on 1st July of the new Victoria Pier. Initially the pier was a very spartan affair providing two deep-water berths until it was extended to its present length in 1885.

*The first **King Orry** was built in Douglas in 1842 but was taken by Napier's shipyard in part payment for the **Douglas** (1).* (Stan Basnett collection)

The iron-hulled **Ben-my-Chree** (1) is seen leaving Douglas. She entered service in 1845 and was fitted with the engines from the **Queen of the Isle**.
(Stan Basnett collection)

The Steam Packet fleet increased to six ships in 1871 when the *King Orry* [2] was launched by R. Duncan & Company of Glasgow. Four years later the *Ben-my-Chree* [2] was built by the Barrow Shipbuilding Company. The 1,000 gross ton mark was passed for the first time as the new 'Ben' had a gross tonnage of 1,030 but she was a slow vessel capable of only 14 knots, this being two knots slower than her original contract speed.

The new pier at Llandudno opened in May 1877 and provided a deep-water berthing head making it more practical to provide sailings to the Welsh resort.

The supremacy of the paddle steamer was first challenged in the Steam Packet fleet by the completion of the *Mona* [2] in 1878. She was a single-screw steamer launched from Laird Brothers' yard at Birkenhead in May 1878 and attained 12.5 knots on her trials. The *Mona* was much more economical to run than the paddle steamers and was better suited to the winter service.

The **Tynwald** (1) followed the first 'Ben' into service in 1846 and served for twenty years with the Company. (Manx Museum)

*The **Snaefell** (1) was a product of Caird & Co. of Greenock. She was sold on to the Zeeland Steamship Company in 1875.* (Manx Museum)

The last iron ship and the first twin-screw steamer in the fleet was the *Fenella* [1] launched in June 1881 by the Barrow Shipbuilding Company. However, despite the success of the early screw steamers, the Steam Packet Company ordered a large paddle steamer from Caird & Company of Greenock in 1881. She was named *Mona's Isle* [3] and achieved 18.18 knots on trials.

In 1882 the hull of the *Mona's Isle* [2] was considered sound enough to warrant her conversion to a twin-screw steamer and this work was undertaken by Westray, Copeland & Company at Barrow-in-Furness. Her name was changed to *Ellan Vannin* and she became associated with services from Ramsey.

When the *Mona* [2] was at anchor near the Mersey Bar

*This famous picture is believed to be one of the earliest taken of a Steam Packet ship. It shows the arrival at Douglas of the new Lieutenant Governor Francis Piggot and his family on board the **Tynwald** (1) on 14th February 1861.* (Stan Basnett collection)

*The **Snaefell** (2) at Steam Packet berth in Ramsey inner harbour, which was tidal. She served the Company from 1876 until 1904. (Midwood/Stan Basnett collection)*

lightship on 5th August 1883, the Spanish steamer *Rita* ran into her. The *Mona* sank in half an hour and all her crew and two passengers were picked up by the tug *Conqueror*. To replace the sunken vessel the Company ordered the *Peveril* [1] from the Barrow Shipbuilding Company.

During 1884 the *Ben-my-Chree* [2] was reboilered. Two additional funnels were fitted so that she had a total of four: two forward of the paddle boxes and two aft. Although she now looked one of the most impressive vessels which the Steam Packet

Company has ever operated, the new boilers did little to increase her slow speed of only 14 knots.

With the entry into service of the *Mona's Queen* [2] in 1885 the Steam Packet fleet increased to ten vessels.

In 1887 a rival concern styled the Isle of Man, Liverpool and Manchester Steamship Company built the paddle steamers *Queen Victoria* and *Prince of Wales*. Both these ships were faster by half an hour than any Steam Packet vessel on the Liverpool and Douglas route. Competition became fierce and in 1888 both companies

*The **Mona's Isle** (3) on Scarlett Point in 1892. She was stranded for two days before being assisted off the rocks by the **Tynwald** (3). (Manx Museum)*

*The ill-fated screw ship **Ellan Vannin** was built as the **Mona's Isle** (2) in 1860. She sank with all hands at the Mersey Bar in December 1909. (Manx Museum)*

*A splendid study of the **Snaefell** (2) rolling in a stiff breeze as she leaves Ramsey and still flying the 'Blue Peter' from her foremast.*(Southward/Stan Basnett collection)

The third **Mona** came third-hand to the Company. Built as the **Calais-Douvres** in 1889 for the London, Chatham & Dover's Railway's Dover-Calais service, she came to the Steam Packet from Liverpool & Douglas Steamers to whom she had been sold in 1900. She was only to serve for six years before she was broken-up in 1909. (Jeffrey D. Sankey collection)

*The **Peveril** (1) entered service in 1884, her career being cut short when she was sunk in a collision off Douglas in 1899. She is seen leaving the harbour at Ramsey.*
(Stan Basnett collection)

were involved in a price-cutting war. The fares of the Manx Line, as the new company was popularly known, were reduced to 5/- (25p) First Class and 2/6d (12.5p) Second Class. The wholly uneconomic practice of racing was reintroduced with the rival steamers leaving Liverpool or Douglas at identical times. In November 1888 both the *Queen Victoria* and the *Prince of Wales* were sold to the Steam Packet Company. With the acquisition of the two new steamers the

Douglas [2] and the *Tynwald* [2] were effectively redundant and were sold for breaking-up in January 1889.

In 1887 the Steam Packet Company purchased the Imperial Hotel on the quay at Douglas and, until 1969, established its headquarters there. Passenger traffic was on the rapid increase towards the end of the century and 516,359 passengers were carried in 1894. This was an increase of 230,000 on the total of

*The **Ben-my-Chree** (2) was the most distinctive of all Steam Packet ships following her re-boilering in 1884 when she was fitted with two extra funnels.*
(Manx Museum)

The **Fenella** (1) was built at Barrow in 1881and remained in service until 1929. (Manx Museum)

The **King Orry** (2) paddling purposefully towards Douglas at the close of a routine voyage from Liverpool. (Liverpool Maritime Museum)

175

The **Tynwald** (2) of 1866 served the Company for 23 years.. It is low water at Douglas as the ship sits at the Red Pier waiting for the tide. (Ferry Publications Library)

The **Prince of Wales** was one of a pair of powerful steamers purchased from the rival Liverpool & Manchester SS Co. (Manx Line) in 1888. (Manx Museum)

32

*The magnificent **Empress Queen** was the largest and fastest paddle steamer ever built for the Steam Packet and entered service in 1897. A product of the Fairfield yard, she was wrecked on Bembridge Ledge (Isle of Wight) whilst trooping in 1916. (Manx Museum)*

ten years earlier. A spate of opposition companies was encountered in the 1890s but nothing as serious as the Manx Line emerged.

The Diamond Jubilee year of Queen Victoria saw the launch of the magnificent paddle steamer *Empress Queen* from the Fairfield yard at Govan on 14th March 1897. She achieved 21.75 knots on trials and the following year was averaging 3 hours 5 minutes for the Liverpool - Douglas passage.

The *Peveril* [1] sank off Douglas on 17th September 1899 following a collision with the coaster *Monarch*. The *Peveril's* crew and one passenger were transferred to the *Monarch* and were landed at Douglas.

*The **Ramsey** was built at Barrow-in-Furness and could carry up to 1,162 passengers. She was lost in the First World War.*
(Stan Basnett collection)

*The trim little **Tynwald** (3) was built at Govan in 1891 and was for many years the Ardrossan steamer. She was sold out of service in 1933 but was not broken up until 1952. (John Clarkson collection)*

CHAPTER THREE

The Years of Plenty 1900 – 1913

1900: *Relief of Mafeking, Boer War, 28th February*

1901: *Queen Victoria died, 22nd January*

1902: *Visit to IOM of King Edward VII and
Queen Alexandra, 24th August*

1903: *First flight in 'heavier-than-air machine',
Wright Brothers', Kitty Hawk*

1904: *IOM Railway purchased Manx Northern and
Foxdale lines for £67,000*

1909: *Peary reached North Pole. Bleriot made first
cross-Channel flight*

1910: *Accession of King George V on death of Edward VII*

1911: *Amundsen reached South Pole, 14th December*

1912: Titanic *disaster off Cape Race, 14th April*

At the turn of the century, the Isle of Man Steam Packet was operating a fleet of eleven vessels which comprised eight paddle steamers and three twin-screw steamers. The oldest was the *Ellan Vannin* (built as the *Mona's Isle* [2] in 1860), and the newest was the *Empress Queen* of 1897.

Some fairly stiff opposition was being encountered from Liverpool & Douglas Steamers (formed in 1899) and a price-cutting war was in progress. In 1900 a First Class saloon return was available at 4/- (20p).

Until 1901 all the Steam Packet Company's ships had been ordered by and built for the Company, with the exception of the *Queen Victoria* and *Prince of Wales*, purchased from the Manx Line in 1888. However, a replacement was needed for the *Peveril* [1], lost in 1899, and so in 1901 the Company purchased the 813-ton

Alongside at Ramsey is the steamer **Peveril** *(1). Her presence in the harbour has attracted a good crowd of sight-seers.* (Midwood/Stan Basnett collection)

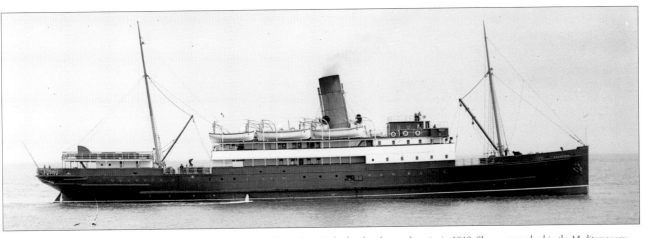

The **Snaefell** (3) was the first Steam Packet ship to come from Cammell Laird's at Birkenhead and entered service in 1910. She was torpedoed in the Mediterranean eight years later. (Jeffrey D. Sankey collection)

single-screw steamer *Dora* from the London & South Western Railway Company. She was quickly renamed *Douglas* [3].

On 28th June 1902, the Coronation of King Edward VII was marked by a Review of the Fleet at Spithead. On this occasion the *Mona's Isle* [3] was chartered to Lunn's for a special cruise from Southampton Docks.

In December 1902, Liverpool & Douglas Steamers went into liquidation and the following year the Steam Packet Company purchased the former Dover Strait vessel *Calais-Douvres* from the liquidators for £6,000 and renamed her *Mona* [3]. Built in 1889, this vessel became the final paddle steamer to be added to the Manx fleet.

The *Empress Queen* was fitted with Marconi 'wireless' in 1903

and was the first Steam Packet ship to be so equipped. The total number of passengers carried in 1903 amounted to 711,514 and the standard return fare was 10/- (50p).

In 1904 the Isle of Man received its first visit from a steam turbine vessel. The Midland Railway Company's *Londonderry* operated an excursion sailing from the newly- opened port of Heysham on 13th August. Two months prior to this the railway company had launched the turbine steamer *Manxman* and with such a name she was obviously destined to provide a rival service. On 1st June 1905 the *Manxman* inaugurated the service, the afternoon crossing from Heysham to Douglas being scheduled to take just 2 hours 40 minutes.

The second **Mona's Queen** was the Steam Packet's last operational paddle steamer and finally passed for breaking in 1929. (John Clarkson collection)

To counter this opposition, the Isle of Man Steam Packet Company placed an order with Armstrong, Whitworth & Company of Newcastle-upon-Tyne for a new direct-drive turbine steamer which would be guaranteed to steam at least three-quarters of a knot faster than the *Manxman*. This was the Steam Packet's first turbine steamer, and the only vessel ever to be built for them on the north-east coast. She was named *Viking* at her launch on 7th March 1905 and on her trials achieved 23.53 knots. The *Viking* became the mainstay of the Douglas - Fleetwood service on which she would burn up to 60 tons of coal a day. On 25th May 1907 she crossed from Fleetwood to Douglas in 2 hours 22 minutes, a record that stood until the introduction of SeaCat services in June 1994.

The success of the *Viking* prompted the Company to order a larger turbine steamer from the Barrow yard of Vickers, Sons & Maxim Limited. She was launched on 23rd March 1908 and named *Ben-my-Chree* [3]. Direct-drive turbines coupled to triple screws gave a trials speed of 24.26 knots. The new 'Ben' had a passenger certificate for 2,549, carried a crew of 119 and could burn 95 tons of coal in one day's steaming. On 9th July 1909 the *Ben-my-Chree* made her fastest recorded passage from Liverpool to Douglas, berth to berth, in 2 hours 57 minutes.

On 3rd December 1909 the *Ellan Vannin* left Ramsey for Liverpool at 01.13 with 15 passengers, 21 crew, mail and 60 tons of cargo. A severe north-westerly gale blew up whilst she was on passage, and as the steamer approached the Mersey Bar lightship at about 06.45 the gale reached storm force. In what was to

become the worst peacetime disaster ever to befall the Company, the *Ellan Vannin* foundered between the lightship and the Q.1 buoy at about 07.00. She is believed to have been swept by heavy seas and broached to, sinking by the stern. All aboard were lost. Later the same day lifebuoys, bags of turnips and a piano were seen floating near the Formby lightship but it was not until 8th December that the first bodies were washed ashore.

The subsequent Board of Trade Enquiry into the disaster had no direct evidence available to form an opinion as to the precise cause. The Enquiry found that the ship was in good order and there were no criticisms of the Company, Master or crew.

On 12th February 1910 the *Snaefell* [3] was launched at Birkenhead. She was the first Steam Packet ship to be built by Cammell Laird & Company (the *Mona* [2] was built by Laird Brothers). The new *Snaefell* was extensively used on the Liverpool to Douglas winter service.

In 1911 the railway-operated Fleetwood overnight steamers *Duke of York* and *Duke of Lancaster* were purchased by Turkish interests and sent to Cammell Laird at Birkenhead for complete refurbishment. The deal with the Turks fell through and the Isle of Man Steam Packet Company purchased both these vessels. The *Duke of Lancaster* was renamed *The Ramsey* and the *Duke of York* became the *Peel Castle*.

A new *King Orry* [3] was launched at Cammell Laird's, Birkenhead on 11th March 1913 to replace the 1871 paddle steamer of the same name. The ship's sponsor, Miss Waid, was rather startled at the launching ceremony when the ship began to

*The **King Orry** (3) served the Steam Packet from 1913 until her loss during the Dunkirk evacuation in 1940. (John Clarkson collection)*

*The **Ben-my-Chree** (3), dressed overall and approaching the Victoria Pier, was to become one of the best-loved of all Manx steamers.* (John Clarkson collection)

move down the slipway before she had finished her speech! This was the first geared turbine steamer in the fleet - these had proved to be more economical than direct-drive.

In 1913, such was the boom in Manx tourism that the total number of passengers carried by the Isle of Man Steam Packet Company rose to 1,152,048. This represented the vast proportion of visitors to the Isle of Man, but the Midland Railway Company's Heysham-Douglas service and the Liverpool & North Wales Steamship Company's Llandudno-Douglas service would have increased the total.

*The splendid **Viking** of 1905 was the Steam Packet's first turbine steamer and served during both World Wars, not passing for scrap until her 49th season.* (IOMSP Co Ltd)

CHAPTER FOUR

The Great War 1914 – 1918

175

1914: Archduke Francis Ferdinand assassinated at Sarajevo, 28th June

1915: Sinking of the Cunard steamer Lusitania *by German U20, 7th May*

1916: Republican rising in Ireland, 24th April

1916: Battle of Jutland, 31st May

1917: British victory on Passchendaele Ridge, 4th October

1918: British Naval raid on Zeebrugge, 23rd April

1918: Armistice signed by Germans, 11th November

The First World War began on 4th August in what should have been the peak of the Steam Packet Company's summer seasonal traffic. Passenger arrivals over the first weekend in August fell away drastically and at a special meeting of the Directors on 10th August it was decided to lay up the *Ben-my-Chree* [3], the *Viking* and the *Empress Queen* with immediate effect.

By the end of October 1914 the *King Orry*, *Peel Castle*, *The Ramsey* and the *Snaefell* had all been requisitioned by the Admiralty which had also asked for plans of all five of the Company's paddle steamers. From fifteen vessels at the outbreak of the war, the Steam Packet's fleet was reduced to four within a

Robert Lloyd's fine painting of the **King Orry** *(3) shows her at the surrender of the German High Seas Fleet east of the Firth of Forth in November 1918. This event represented one of the Steam Packet's greatest hours and the painting is now reproduced as a Manx Post Office stamp. (By kind permission of Stan Basnett)*

The **Viking** became the seaplane carrier HMS **Vindex** during the First World War. (Imperial War Museum)

The **Peel Castle** was built as the Lancashire & Yorkshire Railway's **Duke of York** in 1894 and was purchased by the Steam Packet in 1912. (Imperial War Museum)

175

few months. The *Douglas, Tynwald, Fenella* and *Tyrconnel* remained to maintain the wartime services - they were all small screw steamers, each of under 1,000 tons.

The number of passengers carried in 1914 dropped by almost two-thirds of the 1913 total to just 404,481.

The Steam Packet Company's five paddle steamers and two large turbine steamers were pressed into war service early in 1915. The *Prince of Wales* had her name changed to *Prince Edward* to avoid confusion with the battleship.

The *Viking* and the *Ben-my-Chree* were both converted to carry seaplanes. A hangar was built aft of the second funnel to house six seaplanes which would be lifted in and out of the water by a crane.

There was a once popular story that the 'Ben' was loaded with ammunition and sent round the Cape of Good Hope to service warships that were under orders to sink the German light cruiser *Königsberg* which was sheltering in the River Rufiji in Tanganyika

(Tanzania). She is said to have made this long journey, from England to East Africa, at an average speed in excess of 22 knots, including stops for coaling. However, as surviving log fragments have shown, it would have been impossible for her to have made the trip between her North Sea operations and her main Mediterranean war work.

On 7th August 1915 HMS *Ramsey* (ex *The Ramsey*) left Scapa Flow in the Orkney Islands. Next day, when she was in the south-east approach to the Pentland Firth, she challenged a supposedly Russian ship which turned out to be the German minelaying raider *Meteor. The Ramsey* was fired on at short range and sank rapidly with very heavy loss of life after a torpedo from the *Meteor* had shattered her stern. Fifty-two of the *Ramsey's* crew were killed, and forty-six were picked up by the raider.

The *King Orry* struck a submerged reef in the Sound of Islay when she was steaming at 19 knots on 9th June 1915. Using the hand steering gear, and with only the port turbines working, she

The **Mona's Queen** (2) in full dazzle paint and berthed in Weymouth Harbour during the First World War. (John Clarkson collection)

*During the First World War the **King Orry** (3) served as an armed boarding vessel at Scapa Flow.* (Imperial War Museum)

proceeded to Birkenhead for repairs by Cammell Laird.

At Easter 1916 the *Tynwald* [3] made trooping trips to Kingstown (Dun Laoghaire) in connection with the suppression of the Irish rebellion.

Whilst inward bound to Southampton from Le Havre at 05.00 on 1st February 1916, the *Empress Queen* stranded on Bembridge Ledge, Isle of Wight. Visibility was only a few metres with light airs and a smooth sea. She ran aground on a rising tide and the 1,300 troops on board were taken off by destroyers. It was not expected to be a difficult job to tow her off but, after several attempts had failed, a severe gale blew up and she became a total loss.

On 11th January 1917 the *Ben-my-Chree* was anchored in a supposedly safe bay off the island of Castellorizo (off the south-west Mediterranean coast of Turkey). However, the surrounding hills were occupied by Turks who opened fire, igniting petrol and holing the ship which sank in shallow water. The 'Ben' was

*The **Snaefell** (3) on Admiralty duties prior to her loss in June 1918.* (Imperial War Museum)

abandoned after half an hour, and her crew of 250 were able to get safely ashore with only four wounded. The Master and the Chief Engineer later returned to the 'Ben' and saved the ship's cat and two dogs.

On 6th February 1917 the *Mona's Queen* [2] left Southampton under the command of Captain Cain with 1,000 troops on board, bound for Le Havre. Some twenty miles from the French coast a German U-Boat surfaced almost dead ahead. The 'Queen' kept on course, despite a torpedo being fired at her, and the U-Boat's conning tower was struck by her port paddle-box, the steel paddle floats inflicting severe damage. Despite diving immediately the U-Boat (UC.26) was not fatally wounded and arrived at Ostend two days later for repairs and overhaul. UC.26 was finally sunk in the Thames estuary by the Royal Navy on 30th April 1917.

The *Mona's Queen* was disabled by the incident but managed to steam slowly into Le Havre. After discharging her troops she steamed back to Southampton for repairs at Harland & Wolff and resumed her trooping duties on 17th March.

The *King Orry* [3] had the distinction of following the light cruiser HMS *Cardiff* and 14 German capital ships at the surrender of the German High Seas Fleet, forty miles east of the Island of May at the entrance to the Firth of Forth, on 21st November 1918.

In December 1918 the Isle of Man Steam Packet Company's fleet consisted of the *Fenella* [1], *Tynwald* [3] and *Douglas* [3] available for service, and the *Mona's Queen* [2], *Peel Castle* and *King Orry* [3] under requisition, in addition to the cargo steamer *Tyrconnel*. The two principal passenger carriers the *Ben-my-Chree* [3] and the *Empress Queen* had been lost, as had the *Snaefell* [3] and *The Ramsey*. The *Prince of Wales* and the *Queen Victoria* were not worth reconditioning, nor was the *Mona's Isle* [3]. The *Viking* was purchased back from the Admiralty.

CHAPTER FIVE

The Inter-War Years 1919 – 1939

175

1919: First direct flight across the Atlantic by Alcock and Brown, 15th June

1920: Visit to IOM of King George V and Queen Mary who arrived at Ramsey

1921: Irish Free State established, 6th December

1926: General Strike in Britain

1928: Visit of 14 seater airliner from Croydon raised prospect of regular air services to the Island

1929: IOM in direct telephone contact with England, 26th June

1933: Loch Promenade in Douglas widened from Victoria Pier to War Memorial

1936: King Edward VIII Pier at Douglas opened – cost £212,000, 24th May

1936: King Edward VIII abdicated after a reign of 325 days, 10th December

1938: Munich Agreement between Chamberlain, Hitler and Mussolini, 29th September

1939: British Fleet mobilised, 31st August

*The **Mona** (4) was originally Laird Line's **Hazel** of 1907 and was purchased by the Steam Packet for £65,000 in 1919 to replace war losses.* (John Clarkson collection)

An unusual and important problem faced the Isle of Man Steam Packet Company at the end of the war. The fleet of steamers was dispersed and could only be brought back to pre-war standards at considerable cost. In February 1919 the Company had a capital of £200,000 in £1 shares and had more than £700,000 in investments, plus a fleet which had been written down to a book value of under £70,000. The Company had received more than £500,000 from chartering fees, payments for loss of steamers and awards from underwriters.

At the Company's Annual General Meeting some of the Directors argued that it would be perfectly possible to wind up

This photograph taken from the Peveril Hotel shows the Victoria Pier and the building affectionately known as 'The Triangle' with its ornate clock tower. It was replaced by the present terminal building in 1961. (Manx Museum)

*The **King Orry** (3) became something of a tourist attraction after she had run aground at New Brighton in August 1921. (John Clarkson collection)*

*The **Mona's Isle** (4) was the second Dover-based vessel to transfer to the Steam Packet. Built at Dumbarton as the **Onward** in 1905, the turbine steamer was purchased in 1920 and served for part of her first season at Douglas with her original name. (John Clarkson collection)*

the Company if the shareholders so wished, and £5 could be paid out for every £1 of the issued capital. A group of shareholders did in fact propose that the Directors should either offer to sell the Company to the Manx Government or dispose of it as a going concern. The Chairman led a counter-attack and proposed that the Company should carry on, this proposal being approved.

The fleet in 1919 had a total passenger capacity of less than 10,000: in 1914 this figure was in excess of 20,000. Yet with the return of the holiday trade in 1919, incoming passenger arrivals were 343,332.

*The **Manx Maid** (1) was purchased by the Steam Packet in 1923 having previously been the Channel Islands steamer **Caesarea** of 1910. (John Clarkson collection)*

The Company started to replace the depleted fleet by purchasing the *Hazel* from the Laird Line in January 1919. She had been built at Govan in 1907 for the Ardrossan - Portrush service which was not restarted after the war. The *Hazel* was renamed *Mona* [4].

The *Mona's Queen* [2] was refitted by Cammell Laird in April 1919 and was available for the summer season. The *King Orry* [3] had a period of trooping between Southampton and French ports but returned to Cammell Laird early in 1919 for complete refurbishment and was back on Steam Packet service in July. The *Peel Castle* sailed as a troopship until May 1919 after which she was returned to the Company.

In order to boost the passenger capacity of the fleet for the 1919 summer season the elderly paddle steamer *La Marguerite* was chartered from the Liverpool & North Wales Steamship Company from 28th June to 16th September. With her passenger certificate for 2,077 she was extensively used for the period of the charter.

The Isle of Man Steam Packet Company purchased the Midland Railway Company's turbine steamer *Manxman* from the Admiralty and sent her to Barrow for a complete refit in February 1920. In an attempt to replace the *Ben-my-Chree* [3], lost in 1917, the *Manxman* was placed on the principal Liverpool - Douglas route. The *Viking*, which had survived the war, was back on the Fleetwood - Douglas service in June 1920.

Another purchase of second-hand tonnage was made in March 1920 when the Company bought the *Viper* from G. & J. Burns of

After the war the **Peel Castle** was recommissioned and served the Company until 1939. (Bruce Peter collection)

The **Viking** was latterly associated with the Fleetwood service although this view shows her leaving Ardrossan on the Firth of Clyde. (Bruce Peter collection)

Glasgow. She had been built in 1906 for the Ardrossan - Belfast daylight service and was renamed *Snaefell* [4] for her Manx service.

A third purchase was made in 1920 when the 1905-built Dover Strait steamer *Onward* was acquired. Her name was eventually changed to *Mona's Isle* [4].

In 1920 the Steam Packet Company's fleet carried a total of 1,094,220 passengers. This fleet was a rather motley collection of thirteen vessels and there was no 'crack' ship. Only five had been built for the Company, the remaining eight having been brought in second-hand. Just one paddle steamer remained - the *Mona's Queen* [2] of 1885, and it was an elderly fleet with an average age of 22 years. This state of affairs was set to continue for almost a decade until the Company's new building programme commenced with the *Ben-my-Chree* [4] of 1927.

The salvage steamer *Valette* raised the wreck of the *Ben-my-Chree* [3] at Castellorizo in 1920 and the hulk was towed to Piraeus. Following examination, repairs were not considered possible.

In 1921 the *Manxman*'s boilers were adapted for burning oil fuel which enabled her to keep sailing throughout the coal strike of 1926. She was the first Steam Packet ship to be so treated.

In November 1923 the Company made another second-hand purchase when it bought the Southampton-based *Caesarea* from the Southern Railway Company. Earlier that year the vessel had struck rocks off St Helier, Jersey. The Steam Packet Company arranged for her to be towed to Barrow for refurbishment and she was converted to burn oil fuel. The *Caesarea* was renamed *Manx Maid* [1] and commenced on the Company's sailings in Summer 1924.

The major strikes of 1926 disrupted the Steam Packet's operations. The coal-burning units all had empty bunkers and passenger arrivals at Douglas slumped by 156,000. The main Liverpool - Douglas route was maintained by the two oil-burners *Manxman* and *Manx Maid*. From 20th May 1926 sailings between Liverpool and Douglas were reduced to a single passage each way daily.

The new *Ben-my-Chree* [4] was launched by Cammell Laird at Birkenhead on 5th April 1927. Construction had been rapid - the keel had been laid just over four months earlier in November 1926. Cammell Laird had been promised a bonus of £2,000 if they could meet the delivery date of 25th June 1927. The new 'Ben' achieved 22.8 knots on her trials and her passenger capacity was for 2,586, by a coincidence the same figure as her gross

The launch of the new flagship **Ben-my-Chree** (4) at Birkenhead in 1927 began a remarkable career. She was such a popular ship that many Fleet Commodores preferred her to the Company's centenary steamer, the **Lady of Mann** (1).(Wirral Archives)

The new 'Ben' is seen on official speed trials in the Firth of Clyde and looks every inch a flier. (Wirral Archives)

tonnage. In July 1927 Cammell Laird reported a loss of £17,000 on building the 'Ben'. The Steam Packet paid £192,000 and then agreed to round up the figure to £200,000. The 'Ben' was the Company's first new ship since 1913 and the first to be built as an oil-burner.

In 1928 the Steam Packet Company took over the Heysham - Douglas service from the Midland Railway Company and had a virtual monopoly of the Manx passenger traffic for the next 41 years. Two vessels were purchased from the railway company: the *Duke of Cornwall* of 1898 which was renamed *Rushen Castle*, and the *Antrim* of 1904 which was renamed *Ramsey Town*.

A third additional steamer was added to the fleet in 1928. She was the Southern Railway Company's *Victoria* built in 1907 and was a younger sister of the *Mona's Isle* [4], ex *Onward*. The

Victoria retained her original name throughout her Steam Packet service.

The Isle of Man Steam Packet Company's fleet in 1928 consisted of seventeen steamers. At one end of the scale the new 'crack' steamer *Ben-my-Chree* was just one year old, whilst at the other end of the scale the *Fenella* [1] was still steaming after 47 years. The total age of the fleet amounted to 440 years, giving an average age of 26 years, four more than in 1920. The last paddle steamer, the *Mona's Queen* [2] of 1885, remained in service.

A specially designed cargo vessel was launched from Cammell Laird's yard in 1929 and named *Peveril* [2]. Early on in her career she was passing through the Brunswick Lock at Liverpool when the swing bridge operated prematurely and removed her mainmast! The end of the 1929 summer season turned out to be a

The **Rushen Castle** *was originally the Lancashire & Yorkshire Railway's* **Duke of Cornwall** *of 1898. The Steam Packet purchased her in 1928 and she survived in Manx service until 1946.* (John Clarkson collection)

THE INTER-WAR YEARS 1919-1939

*The **Manxman** was another inter-war purchase. She was built for the Midland Railway's new Heysham services in 1904 and was a regular visitor to Douglas. She eventually passed to the Steam Packet in 1920 without a change of name.* (John Clarkson collection)

time for farewells. The Company's last paddle steamer, the *Mona's Queen* [2], made her final passenger sailing from Fleetwood to Douglas; the *Fenella* [1] completed her last voyage from Workington to Douglas and the *Tynwald* [3], after spending the summer operating cruises from Blackpool's North Pier, was laid up at Barrow. The number of passengers carried on the Company's steamers in 1929 totalled 1,177,799.

On 3rd July 1929 the Company placed an order with the newly-formed shipbuilding company Vickers-Armstrong Limited at Barrow for a new passenger steamer. She was launched as the *Lady of Mann* on 4th March to celebrate the centenary of the Isle of Man Steam Packet Company. In her first years of service the 'Lady' had a passenger certificate for 2,873.

In the spring of 1932 the *Ben-my-Chree* was chartered to take a

sailing to the Eucharistic Conference being held in Dublin and it was thought appropriate to paint her hull white for the occasion. For the sum of just £63, Vickers-Armstrong carried out this work. The 'Ben's' white hull was very favourably received and the *Lady of Mann* was painted white in time for the 1933 summer season.

The Steam Packet Company returned to Cammell Laird at Birkenhead for its next new steamer and the *Mona's Queen* [3] was launched in April 1934 with a white hull and green boot topping. In the 'Ben' of 1927, the 'Lady' of 1930 and the new 'Queen', the Company had perhaps the finest short-sea ships in the world, as well as offering a service second-to-none.

In March 1936 two new vessels were ordered from Vickers-Armstrong at Barrow. A double launch took place on 16th December 1936 when the *Fenella* [2] and the *Tynwald* [4] entered

*The Company's centenary ship the **Lady of Mann** (1) going down the ways at Barrow in March 1930.* (Jeffrey D.Sankey)

*The **Ramsey Town** was originally the Midland Railway's steamer **Antrim** which was built for the new Heysham - Belfast overnight service in 1904. The Steam Packet acquired her in 1928 and retained her in service for another eight years.* (John Clarkson collection)

*The third **Mona's Queen** (3) was built at Birkenhead in 1934 and was an altogether larger ship with an extra deck which made her a more awkward vessel to handle. This trials view shows her at her best at speed, with a white hull and showing her graceful counter stern. (John Clarkson collection)*

*The **Ben-my-Chree's** (4) hull was painted white in 1932 after the Board decided it would improve the image of the Company. (John Clarkson collection)*

Mona's Queen (3)

Above: *The **Mona's Queen (3)** under construction at Cammell Laird's. This bird's-eye view gives a good impression of the ship's layout and her long, lean hull.*

Top right: *The **Mona's Queen** goes down the ways at Birkenhead after her naming ceremony on 12th April 1934.*

Middle right: *The First Class Ladies' Lounge.*

Bottom right: *The First Class Dining Room was situated forward on the extra Forecastle Deck which must have been an uncomfortable place to eat in any weather.*

(All pictures Wirral Archives)

*A fine study of a pristine-looking **Ben-my-Chree** (4), ready to take up service shortly before the Second World War at Barrow. (Jeffrey D.Sankey)*

The **Victoria** of 1907 was a sister of the **Onward/ Mona's Isle** (4) and joined the Steam Packet from the Southern Railway in 1928. Converted to oil burning later in her career, this remarkable vessel saw 49 years' service and was not broken up until her fiftieth. She was the Steam Packet's last two-funnelled steamer in service. (Bruce Peter collection)

the water. The new ships were specifically designed for the winter services and were the forerunners of the 1946 'King Orry class'which were so familiar until the early 1980s. Although turbine steamers, both the new ships were given squat funnels with horizontal tops which were the fashion of the new motor ships of the 1930s but which, in the view of this writer, greatly detracted from their otherwise fine lines.

In March 1937 the Manx Government grudgingly agreed to Sunday excursionists and the new *Tynwald* inaugurated special Sunday sailings. In the summer of 1937 the Isle of Man Steam Packet Company was operating a total of eighteen steamers, the highest number in its history and a fleet total never to be exceeded.

The *King Orry* was converted to burn oil fuel in time for the 1939 summer season. In that final summer before the outbreak of war, the *Ben-my-Chree* was rostered to provide a series of particularly attractive excursion sailings from Liverpool to Douglas, every Sunday from 25th June until 20th August. Three hours were allowed ashore and a contract ticket for all nine excursions cost just £1-15s-0d. (£1.75).

The **Tynwald** (4) being warped out of Douglas inner harbour after her winter lay-up in 1938. (Stan Basnett collection)

*An outstanding view of the **King Orry** (3) at speed inward bound to the Isle of Man prior to the outbreak of the Second World War.* (Jeffrey D. Sankey collectio

CHAPTER SIX

The Second World War 1939 – 1945

1939: War declared between Great Britain and Germany, 3rd September

1940: Operation Dynamo – British and Allied troops evacuated from Dunkirk, 26th May – 4th June

1941: H.M.S. Hood sunk by Bismarck, 24th May

1941: Japanese attack on Pearl Harbour, 7th December

1942: Singapore surrenders to the Japanese, 15th February

1942: El Alamein : Allied offensive opened in Egypt, 23rd October

1944: D-Day, the Allied invasion of Europe, 6th June

1945: VE Day, 8th May

1945: Atomic bomb destroyed Hiroshima, 6th August; VJ Day, 15th August

On the outbreak of war on 3rd September 1939 the Isle of Man Steam Packet Company had a fleet of sixteen steamers. The three cargo steamers *Peveril* [2], *Conister* and *Cushag* were retained by the Company and initially the *Rushen Castle* and the *Victoria* were left to maintain the wartime passenger sailings.

The *King Orry*, *Manx Maid* and *Mona's Isle* were converted into armed boarding vessels, and the remaining eight passenger steamers all became personnel carriers and conveyed part of the British Expeditionary Force to France. The old *Tynwald* [3] was moved from Glasgow to the Wallasey Dock, Birkenhead, where she became the accommodation/supply ship HMS *Eastern Isles*.

The principal event of 1940 was Operation Dynamo, the evacuation of troops from Dunkirk, which lasted from 26th May until 4th June. The total number of troops landed in England from

*The **Mona's Queen** (3) was an early war loss when she broke her back after detonating a mine in the approaches to Dunkirk in May 1940. (IOMSP Co Ltd)*

*The **Fenella** (2) embarking troops alongside the East Mole at Dunkirk during the evacuation of May 1940. Enemy bombs exploded alongside her, pushing heavy stone blocks through her hull, causing her engine room to flood and the ship to settle.* (Imperial War Museum)

Dunkirk is generally accepted as 338,226, and of these 24,669 were brought out on the eight steamers of the Isle of Man Steam Packet Company which took part in the operation.

The 29th May 1940 was perhaps the blackest day in the long and honourable history of the Isle of Man Steam Packet Company. At 05.30 the *Mona's Queen* was approaching Dunkirk and when one mile off the port she detonated a magnetic mine which caused her to break her back and sink. Twenty-four of her crew were lost, seventeen of them from the Isle of Man.

Later that same day the *Fenella* was berthed starboard side to the east mole stone jetty at Dunkirk. She had 650 troops on board when a force of German aircraft bombed the pier at 17.00 with such effect that heavy stone blocks crashed into the side of the ship and her engine room flooded, causing her to settle on an even keel. The Liverpool & North Wales Steamship Company's *St Seiriol* rendered all possible assistance.

The 29th May also claimed the *King Orry* which was bombed in the approaches to Dunkirk and was severely damaged. She was ordered to clear the harbour and the approach channel before she sank. Shortly after 02.00 on the morning of 30th May she sank after her engine room flooded.

The Company had lost three of its steamers in just twenty hours.

The *Mona's Isle* was the first ship to leave Dover when Operation Dynamo started and she brought out 2,634 troops in two round trips. The *Manxman* also made two round trips. On the night of 2nd June, after completing three round trips, the *Ben-my-Chree* was in collision off Folkestone which finished her involvement in the operation. The *Lady of Mann* took 4,262 men back to Dover on four crossings from Dunkirk while the *Tynwald* is recorded as making four round trips and bringing out 8,953 troops.

A fortnight after Dunkirk, Operation Ariel commenced - the evacuation of troops from Le Havre, Cherbourg and Brest. On one sailing from Le Havre the *Lady of Mann* carried as many as 5,000 troops. The *Manx Maid* embarked 3,000 troops at Brest - double her normal complement. The *Manxman* was the final troopship to leave Cherbourg, steaming away to safety as the Germans were entering the port area. Rommel described her as 'the cheeky two-funnelled steamer'. Just before the invasion of the Channel Islands

on 1st July 1940, the *Viking* steamed into St Peter Port, Guernsey and took 1,800 children to the safety of Weymouth.

Whilst on passage from Douglas to Liverpool on 20th December 1940, the *Victoria* exploded two mines in her wake but reached port unscathed. When outward bound to Douglas on 27th December and eight miles north-west of the Bar Lightship she detonated another mine which severely disabled her. Fortunately it was flat calm and her 200 passengers were transferred to other vessels. The *Victoria* was towed back to Liverpool. After this incident the Company's passenger operations were transferred to Fleetwood with effect from 28th December 1940.

After her mine damage had been repaired, the *Victoria* did not return to the Company but was requisitioned and fitted out as an LSI (Landing Ship Infantry) before sailing to the Firth of Forth as a target vessel.

In 1941 the *Tynwald* was converted to an auxiliary anti-aircraft cruiser and most of her superstructure was removed. She was commissioned on 1st October and took up convoy escort work in the Western Approaches. The *Mona's Isle* joined the Rosyth Command after refit becoming the A.A. guardship at Methil in the Firth of Forth. From 1941 until the beginning of 1944 the *Ben-my-Chree* was a troop transporter, often sailing as far north as

*The **Mona's Queen** (3) sinking in the approaches to Dunkirk after breaking her back when detonating a magnetic mine.* (Imperial War Museum)

*HMS **Tynwald** (4) as an auxiliary anti-aircraft cruiser in 1941. She was sunk by an Italian submarine in November of the following year - the Company's fourth war loss.* (Imperial War Museum)

Iceland. In October 1941 the Admiralty requisitioned the *Manxman* and she was commissioned in the Royal Navy as HMS *Caduceus*. She was attached to the Naval RDF (Radio Direction Finding) training establishment HMS *Valkyrie* which had been set up in hotels on Douglas promenade.

HMS *Tynwald* took part in the North Africa campaign and was assigned to Operation Torch. She was at anchor in Bougie Bay, 100 miles to the east of Algiers, when the Italian submarine *Argo* attacked her with two torpedoes in the early hours of 12th November 1942. This was the Company's fourth and final war loss.

In January 1944 the *Ben-my-Chree* went to North Shields to be fitted out as an LSI, carrying six landing craft. After this conversion she was in the English Channel, working up for D-Day.

*The **Ben-my-Chree** (4) at Dover on 18th June 1944 transporting the First Release Group of the British Army to England.* (IOMSPCo)

On 6th June the 'Ben' was at Omaha Beach as headquarters ship for the 514th Assault Flotilla. Like the 'Ben', the *Lady of Mann* had been converted to an LSI. On D-Day the 'Lady' was headquarters ship for the 512th Assault Flotilla, responsible for landings on Juno Beach near Courseulles. The *Victoria* was present at the D-Day landings at Arromanches, and for some days after landed American forces on Utah Beach.

With the impending end of the war in Europe, the *Viking* was derequisitioned in May 1945 and was overhauled at Barrow. She returned to the Fleetwood service on 18th June, still with her hull grey but with her Steam Packet funnel colours restored. The *Mona's Isle* re-entered passenger service in July 1945, and on the 'Isle's return to peacetime work the *Snaefell* was withdrawn due to her deteriorating condition. The *Manx Maid* was returned to the Company in March 1945, but was laid up until the 1946 summer season.

The Company's policy of the post-1918 period of buying-in second-hand tonnage was not repeated and when it became reasonable to expect an Allied victory an order was placed with Cammell Laird at Birkenhead for two passenger steamers. With the coming of peace on 8th May 1945 construction was speeded up and the first ship was launched on 22nd November and named *King Orry* [4]. Her design was a development of the 1936 *Fenella* and *Tynwald* and the new ship and her sisters were designed for service throughout the year.

In 1945, prior to the launch of the new *King Orry*, the Steam Packet Company had a fleet of eleven vessels with a total age of 353 years, giving an amazing average age of 32 years. Only four of the fleet had been built to the Company's specifications; the majority of the fleet consisted of second-hand tonnage purchased in the 1920s.

CHAPTER SEVEN

The Post-War Years 1946 – 1961

1952: Accession of Queen Elizabeth II

1953: Hillary and Tensing climbed Everest, 29th May

1953: Coronation of Queen Elizabeth II, 2nd June

1955: Queen Elizabeth II and Prince Philip visited IOM in HMY Britannia, August

1956: Premium Bonds launched, 1st November

1959: USSR Lunik 1 satellite became the first to escape Earth's gravity, 1st January

1960: National Service ended; the farthing abolished, 31st December

1961: Alan Shepherd made first U.S. manned space flight, 5th May

1961: Britain formally applied to join E.E.C., 10th August

The *Lady of Mann* returned to Douglas on 9th March 1946 and was given a civic reception. After partial reconditioning by Cammell Laird she re-entered Steam Packet service on 14th June.

Meanwhile, the new *King Orry* [4] ran her trials on 12th April. Captain J.E. Ronan, for many years a Master with the Company and now retired, recalls her first arrival at Douglas: "Probably the most exciting and vivid moment of that time was when the new *King Orry* arrived from Cammell Laird. Along with the other lads from the *Mona's Isle*, I crossed the King Edward Pier to have a look at this new and beautiful ship. We were still in the aftermath of war with its grim austerities, and it was a most wonderful experience to perceive all those modern furnishings and gadgets, the magic of which in later life, when looking over new ships (and there were many), was never quite recaptured."

*The **Lady of Mann** (1) arriving at the Victoria Pier at Douglas.* (John Clarkson collection)

The **Tynwald** (5) was the third of the post-war sisters from Cammell Laird at Birkenhead, entering service in July 1947. (John Clarkson collection)

The *King Orry* [4] was delivered to the Company on 16th April 1946 and she made her maiden voyage from Liverpool to Douglas two days later. The principal service had been transferred back to Liverpool from Fleetwood only ten days earlier, on 8th April.

The *Ben-my-Chree* arrived back at Birkenhead from her war service on 11th May 1946 and Cammell Laird had her ready to enter passenger service on 6th July. The *Manx Maid* was back in service at Whitsun 1946 after being laid up for a year. The *Viking* appeared for the 1946 summer season on 21st June.

A sister to the new *King Orry*, the *Mona's Queen* [4], was launched from Cammell Laird's on 5th February 1946 and she made her maiden voyage on 26th June. On 14th September the *Rushen Castle* (dating from 1898) made her final crossing for the Company. Throughout 1946 the *Victoria* sailed as a unit of the leave service on her original route from Dover to Calais while the

Manxman was running on the repatriation service from Harwich to the Hook of Holland.

Another new steamer was launched from Cammell Laird on 24th March 1947 as the *Tynwald* [5]. She was very similar to the two earlier post-war new-buildings and entered service on 31st July. The *Victoria* eventually returned to Steam Packet service on 11th June.

The *Mona's Isle* [4] made her final sailings for the Company at the end of the 1947 season and in 1948 she was replaced by the new *Snaefell* [5] which was launched at Birkenhead on 5th March 1948.

The *Manxman*'s contract with the British Government finished in 1949 and she arrived at Barrow on 28th February. The old ship was surveyed with a view to further service but the costs involved outweighed her life expectancy. The ship was broken up at Preston at the end of 1949.

The **Mona's Queen** (4) at her Birkenhead launch on a sunny 5th February 1946. (Wirral Archives)

The **Tynwald** (5) going down the ways in March 1947. (Wirral Archives)

In 1950 the *Ben-my-Chree*'s appearance was altered by the removal of the cowl from her funnel. The 'Ben' had carried a disproportionately tall funnel from 1927 to the completion of her war service when it was shortened as it gave her a tendency to roll heavily. After a break of eleven years, services from Douglas to Dublin recommenced in 1950 while the *Manx Maid*'s final passenger sailings took place on 26th August that year. The fifth of the post-war fleet replacements, the *Mona's Isle* [5], was launched from Cammell Laird's Birkenhead yard on 12th October.

The old *Tynwald* [3] of 1891 / *Western Isles* / *Eastern Isles* left Wallasey Dock on 13th May 1951 and was towed to La Spezia for demolition. A few weeks earlier the new *Mona's Isle* made her maiden voyage on 22nd March. A 'personal best' for the Liverpool and Douglas passage was made by the *King Orry* on 23rd May 1951 when she crossed, berth to berth, in 3 hours 18 minutes.

For many years the Steam Packet's cargo service from Coburg Dock at Liverpool had been operated by the *Conister* [1] and the *Peveril* [2]. A third vessel was often required and the Company frequently chartered suitable ships. However, a new purpose-built cargo vessel was launched at Troon in August 1951. She was the *Fenella* [3] and was the Company's first motor ship, as well as being the first vessel to be built for the Company in Scotland for 54 years.

The Steam Packet's passenger traffic had always been concentrated into summer peaks, and necessitated the Company keeping a large reserve of vessels for summer-only use. Only two

The **Mona's Isle** (5) of 1951 approaching the Liverpool Landing Stage with one of the Cunard Line's Canadian service ships at anchor in the river. (University of Glasgow Archives)

175

passenger vessels were required during the long winter months and usually six units of the fleet would spend almost nine months of every year laid up at Barrow or Birkenhead.

The principal 'peak' was the weekend of the returning T.T. Week race traffic when the entire fleet would operate a shuttle service around the clock, and the other peaks were the last two Saturdays in July and the first three in August. Saturday 2nd August 1952 was a typical busy day. Leaving Liverpool at 00.27 the *King Orry* had 2,160 passengers on board and on a return

*This view taken in the immediate post-war years shows from left to right: The **Manx Maid** (1) on the north side of the Victoria Pier with the **Ben-my-Chree** (4), **King Orry** (4), **Snaefell** (5) and **Victoria** on the south side. The **St. Seiriol** of the Liverpool & North Wales Steamship Company is unusually berthed on the southern viaduct, which was a tidal berth, and the **Lady of Mann** (1) is at the north Edward Pier. (Stan Basnett collection)*

*The **Mona's Isle** (5) maneouvring out into the Mersey at the start of another season on the Irish Sea.* (Ian Collard)

sailing from Douglas at 06.15 she carried 1,900. The 'Orry' departed from Liverpool again at 10.50 with her full complement of 2,160 passengers and the day was rounded off with the 16.00 Douglas to Fleetwood sailing with 1,440 passengers: 7,660 passengers carried on one steamer in 24 hours.

Saturday 31st January 1953 produced one of the worst winter storms of the century. As usual, the *King Orry* was on winter service and left Liverpool at 10.55 with 120 passengers. After passing the Rock Light she met NNW force 12 conditions and her log records 'very heavy broken sea, fierce rain and sleet squalls. Vessel pitching and pounding heavily, shipping much water at times.' (It will be recalled that on this stormy day the British

Railways car ferry *Princess Victoria* sank on passage between Stranraer and Larne with heavy loss of life). The *King Orry* finally berthed at Douglas at 21.55, exactly eleven hours after leaving Liverpool.

Gales from an easterly point always caused problems at Douglas until the new breakwater was completed in the early 1980s. There was no sheltered berth and at high tide a heavy swell would cause vessels to range up and down the pier. In ESE force 9 conditions on 27th January 1954 the *King Orry* sailed direct from Liverpool to Peel and arrived at the sheltered west coast port after a passage of 5 hours 6 minutes. This was the first instance in post-war years of Peel being used as a diversionary port for Douglas.

*Towards the end of her career with the Steam Packet, the **Mona's Queen** (4) was mainly associated with the Fleetwood service but here she is leaving Ardrossan with canvas screens lowered to protect her semi-open decks from bad weather.* (Bruce Peter collection)

King Orry (4)

Above: *The lead ship in the post-war sextet was the* **King Orry** *(4) which entered service in January 1946. This view looking astern from her port bridge wing shows her uncluttered decks and timeless, slatted deck-seats/ life rafts. The barrier immediately forward of the nearest lifeboat divided First and Second Classes.*

Top right: *The basic Second Class accommodation of the Ladies' Lounge.*

Middle right: *The First Class Ladies' Lounge presented a sharp contrast in comfort.*

Right: *The rather spartan atmosphere of the Second Class Restaurant.*

(All pictures Ferry Publications Library/Wirral Archives)

Another Ardrossan view showing the **Tynwald** *(5) arriving from Douglas.* (Bruce Peter collection)

Peel was regularly used in subsequent winters and during the winter of 1978/79 eighteen diversions were made owing to Douglas being unapproachable in easterly gales.

At the age of 49 years, which had included service in both World Wars, the veteran steamer *Viking* made her final sailings on 14th August 1954. She remained a coal burner to her last day and had been the mainstay of the Fleetwood service throughout her career.

The Isle of Man Steam Packet Company completed its immediate post-war rebuilding programme with the launch of the *Manxman* [2] at Birkenhead on 8th February 1955. She was the sixth and last of the 'King Orry' class'. The new ship attracted some criticism in that a] she was not designed as a car ferry, and b] she

had not been fitted with Denny-Brown stabilisers.

In 1955 the Steam Packet's fleet consisted of six fine new steamers, plus the pre-war *Lady of Mann, Ben-my-Chree* and *Victoria*. The passenger fleet could accommodate in excess of 19,000 passengers at any one time.

At the end of the 1956 summer season the faithful *Victoria* made her final passenger sailings on 17th August and was laid up in the Wallasey Dock at Birkenhead. In January 1957, when the old ship was in her fiftieth year, she was towed to Barrow and the breaker's yard. With the passenger fleet reduced to eight steamers, the Company chartered the Liverpool & North Wales Steamship Company's *St Seiriol* on peak Saturdays in 1957 and 1958.

The *Ben-my-Chree*, thirty years old in 1957, spent the greater

The **Snaefell** *(5) entered service in July 1948.* (Bruce Peter collection)

The **Ben-my-Chree** *(4) in her later, modified, state with shortened funnel (without its heavy cowl) and with post-war black hull. Her profile was certainly improved.* (Stan Basnett)

*The **Lady of Mann** (1) was certainly the best-loved of all recent Steam Packet vessels and here she is with whistle blasting as she passes one of her consorts on passage to Liverpool.* (E.D.Lace)

*The **Mona's Isle** (5) rolling uncomfortably to starboard as she approaches Douglas in gale-force conditions. It was always the claim of the Steam Packet that they always sailed, whatever the weather!* (E.D.Lace)

*The **Manxman** (2) of 1955 was the final vessel in the post-war sextet and remained in service until September 1982. (Ian Collard)*

part of the 1957/58 winter in No.5 drydock at Cammell Laird's yard undergoing a major refit following her survey. A year later the *Lady of Mann* received similar attention.

The reliability of the turbine steamers was second-to-none. It was almost possible to set a clock by the comings and goings of the Isle of Man steamers as they passed the Rock Light. However, on 3rd December 1958 the *King Orry* was unable to leave Liverpool due to a burst steam pipe in the engine room. This was the only occasion in a thirty-year career that she was unable to sail on schedule because of mechanical trouble.

At the Company's Annual General Meeting on 24th February 1960 it was announced that an order might be placed for a car ferry vessel. "The matter is under careful and earnest consideration," said Mr J.F. Crellin, Chairman of the Directors. In the event an

*The former **Mona's Queen** sailed to Greece as the **Barrow Queen** in November 1962 before taking up her new career as a cruise vessel. Here she is newly painted with the blue Chandris funnel and its distinctive 'X'. (Liverpool Maritime Museum)*

*The **Tynwald** (5) berthing at Queen's Pier, Ramsey where selected Belfast sailings called until the Pier's closure to steamer traffic in September 1970. (Stan Basnett)*

The Steam Packet cargo ships were a feature of Island life for many years.

Top left: The **Conister** (1) was built as the **Abington** for a Newcastle-based company in 1921 but was purchased by the Steam Packet in 1932. Very many of the Company's Masters started their Captain's careers in her.

Middle: The **Ramsey** was a sturdy little vessel which enjoyed Manx service between 1964 and 1974 when she was sold on.

Bottom: A stirring view of the **Fenella** (3) leaving Douglas. She joined the Company in 1951 having been a product of the Ailsa yard at Troon.

Top right: Prior to roll on - roll off operations, all the local buses were shipped to the Island by the traditional lift on - lift off method.

(All photos W.Corlett/E.D. Lace/Stan Basnett collection)

*The **Ben-my-Chree** (4) in the Mersey at the end of her career. This steamer was towed to Belgian breakers in December1965. (John Clarkson collection)*

order was placed with Cammell Laird in October 1960.

On Tuesday 1st August 1961 the *Lady of Mann* had to return to Liverpool owing to a bomb scare. Two 'phone calls were received by the Liverpool agents of the Company, Thomas Orford & Son, insisting that there was a bomb on the lower deck, and Captain G.R. Kinley was informed. The 'Lady' was approaching the Bar when Captain Kinley decided to return to Liverpool so that the ship could be searched.

The Fleetwood - Douglas service was abandoned at the end of the 1961 summer season as the wooden berth at Fleetwood was in a state of serious disrepair. The *Mona's Queen* sailed on 11th September with flags on her foremast spelling out 'Deeply Regret

Fleetwood Goodbye'. A week later the *Mona's Queen* herself was placed on the sales list. The new car ferry building at Cammell Laird, coupled with the closure of Fleetwood, had made her redundant.

The *King Orry* had been winter steamer from 1946 to 1961, apart from the 1950/51 winter. On the morning of 24th December 1961 she was attempting to enter Douglas in a full easterly gale when a severe gust caught her and she fell very heavily on to the south corner of the Victoria Pier, splintering her main belting. She retired to Cammell Laird for repairs, but in 1962 the new car ferry would supersede her as winter steamer, in partnership with the *Manxman*.

*The **Mona's Queen** (4) was the first of the post-war passenger ships to leave the fleet after the closure of the Fleetwood service in 1961. (John Clarkson collection)*

CHAPTER EIGHT

The Side-Loading Car Ferries 1962 – 1977

1962: Cuban missile crisis, 22nd October

1963: 'Great Train Robbery' - £2.6 million in mailbags stolen, 8th August

1963: U.S. President J.F. Kennedy assassinated, 22nd November

1965 : Manx Radio went 'on air' during TT Week

1965: Sir Winston Churchill died, 24th January

1966: England won World Cup, 20th July

1968: Ramsey and Peel railway lines closed, 6th/7th September

1969: Neil Armstrong and 'Buzz' Aldrin first men on moon, 21st July

1971: United Kingdom converted to decimal currency, 15th February

1973: Summerland fire disaster at Douglas, 2nd August

The Isle of Man Steam Packet Company's first car ferry, the *Manx Maid* [2] was launched from Cammell Laird's yard on 23rd January 1962. The design principle for vehicle loading was simple - a spiral set of ramps at the stern linked with the car deck so that vehicles could be driven on or off at the appropriate level. This overcame the problem of the twenty-foot tidal range at Douglas. At Liverpool the car deck was on the level with the landing stage.

The *Manx Maid*'s maiden voyage was from Liverpool to Douglas on 23rd May 1962. She was the first Steam Packet vessel to be fitted with stabilisers, and although she undoubtedly was a lively seaboat some accounts of rough crossings have been grossly over-sensationalised. In her first season the 'Maid' was used exclusively on the Liverpool - Douglas route.

At the end of 1962 the news broke that the Liverpool & North Wales Steamship Company had gone into voluntary liquidation.

*The start of a new era! The car ferry **Manx Maid** (2) on the stocks and ready for her launch at Birkenhead in January 1962.* (Wirral Archives)

An artist's impression of the new car ferry was used for pre-service publicity purposes. (Wirral Archives)

The Steam Packet Company stepped in to fill the gap and announced a limited Liverpool - Llandudno service for the summer of 1963. The IOMSPCo actually took over the Llandudno - Douglas route in 1962 following the withdrawal of the *St. Seiriol* in September 1961.

The *Mona's Queen* [4] was sold to the Chandris group in October 1962 and sailed out to Piraeus under the name of *Barrow Queen*. After a complete refit, she sailed in the Mediterranean for almost 19 years as the *Fiesta*.

On 14th February 1964 the *Mona's Isle* was on winter service and had been diverted to Peel due to an easterly gale. The following morning she left Peel breakwater at 06.20 and shortly afterwards her stern ran aground on the rocks behind Peel Castle. Two tugs arrived from Liverpool to tow the 'Isle' to Birkenhead for repairs, and the extensive damage kept her out of service until 14th July, leaving the Company short of one ship during T.T. Week.

A new purpose-built cargo vessel, the *Peveril* [3], arrived at Douglas from her builders at Troon on 7th March 1964, and on the following day sailed on her maiden voyage to Liverpool.

The 44-year-old cargo steamer *Conister* (1) was sold for

scrapping in January 1965. To replace her the Ailsa Shipbuilding Company delivered the small cargo vessel *Ramsey*, which arrived at her 'home' port of Ramsey on 28th January.

The final sailing of the *Ben-my-Chree* [4] was from Douglas to Liverpool in the early hours of Monday 13th September 1965. After a leisurely five hour crossing the 'Ben' was laid up in Morpeth Dock, Birkenhead, and the suffix 'II' added, so that the famous name could be given to the Company's second car ferry, building at Cammell Laird's.

The new *Ben-my-Chree* [5] was launched on 10th December 1965. She was the fourteenth (and final) ship to be built for the Steam Packet Company at Birkenhead. She was the Company's last steamer and the last vessel to be built with her passenger accommodation designed for two classes. There was almost an historic meeting on the Mersey that December day for the old 'Ben' should have left Birkenhead for the breakers' yard in Belgium on the same high tide as the new 'Ben' was launched. However, forecast gales delayed the old 'Ben's' departure and it was not until 18th December that she was towed away.

The new *Ben-my-Chree* sailed on her maiden voyage on 10th May 1966. Apart from a few minor differences, she was a repeat

The official launch party admire the **Manx Maid** *(2) as she slips into the Mersey on 23rd January 1962.* (Wirral Archives)

The **Manx Maid's** *launch party with Mrs. A. Alexander, wife of one of the Company's Directors, smashing the celebratory bottle of champagne on the ship's stem.* (Wirral Archives)

Manx Maid (2)

On board the Steam Packet's first car ferry.

Above: *The **Manx' Maid's** car deck looking aft with the turn-table in the foreground, it was used for swinging the cars round to face the correct way for disembarkation..*

Left: *The Second Class Lounge.*

Below: *One of the vessel's comfortable officer's cabins.*

(All pictures IOMSP Co Ltd Archives)

*Following her successful launch, the **Manx Maid** (2) was towed to Cammell Laird's fitting-out yard.* (Wirral Archives)

*So successful was the premier car ferry that a sister, the **Ben-my-Chree** (5), followed in 1966. Here she is at her best on the measured mile during April.* (Wirral Archives)

*Glistening in the afternoon light, the **Ben-my-Chree** (5) sits alongside the south Edward Pier.* (E.D.Lace)

The 'Ben' goes astern out of Douglas in blowy conditions and with her bow rudder at work. (E.D.Lace)

The sisters together at Liverpool's Landing Stage with the **Manx Maid** *taking on bunkers.* (Ian Collard)

of the highly successful *Manx Maid*. On the maiden voyage passengers were invited to inspect the bridge and an excellent 'High Tea' could be taken for 9s.6d. (47.5p).

Four days later the new 'Ben' sailed to Barrow to lay-up for the duration of the 42-day 1966 seamen's strike. The entire Steam Packet fleet was strikebound until 2nd July which resulted in the T.T. motor cycle races being postponed until September of that year.

With effect from 1st January 1967 all the Company's steamers became 'one class' ships for passengers. Considerable savings could be effected by reducing the number of stewards, particularly in the winter months.

Llandudno Pier was not available to the Company in 1967 as the wooden berthing head had fallen into serious disrepair. Whilst not as important as Fleetwood had been, Llandudno nevertheless produced some 30,000 day-trippers every season, and together with the Liverpool to Llandudno sailings provided mid-week

employment for the Company's steamers. Two concrete dolphins (mooring posts) were built over the 1967/68 winter and sailings resumed in summer 1968.

The sea link between Douglas and Fleetwood re-opened on Good Friday 4th April 1969 when Norwest Hovercraft placed the 700 passenger, 1,339 ton *Stella Marina* on the route. A daily round trip, increased to two on Saturdays, was planned. The following year the *Stella Marina* was not available and Norwest purchased the elderly *Norwest Laird* (ex David MacBrayne's *Lochiel*) for the service. After thirty years on the Islay route the old ship was worn out; she took six hours on passage and only fourteen round trips were completed during the season.

It was announced in late August 1970 that Ramsey's Queens Pier would be closed to passengers at the end of the season as the wooden berthing head was in very poor condition. In 1906 over 36,000 passengers were embarked or landed at Ramsey Pier but by 1969 this had fallen to just 3,054. The final occasion on which

The Stranraer - Larne car ferry **Caledonian Princess** *paying a charter visit to Douglas in June 1967 and berthed astern of the* **Ben-my-Chree** *(5) on the Victoria Pier.* (Ian Collard)

The **Manx Maid** *turns in the inner harbour in the late afternoon sun for Liverpool in July 1982.* (John Hendy)

a Steam Packet vessel called at the pier was on 10th September 1970 when the *Manxman* berthed alongside on a Belfast sailing.

Arguably the Steam Packet's most famous steamer, the magnificent *Lady of Mann* of 1930, was nearing the end of her career in 1971. The 'Lady's' final passenger sailing was from Ardrossan to Douglas on the afternoon of Sunday 14th August and she left Douglas for the last time at 17.00 on 17th August on her way to Barrow to lay up, pending sale. In perfect weather the piers and promenades were lined with several thousand people who wished the old ship an emotional farewell as she swept past the harbour entrance to the accompaniment of her triple-chime whistle. The 'Lady' was purchased by Arnott Young of Dalmuir for demolition and she arrived there on the last day of 1971 under tow of the tug *Wrestler*.

The port of Fleetwood re-opened to Manx steamers on 25th August 1971. A new berth was available and the *Mona's Isle* was rostered to open the new service.

In Summer 1971 there had been an acute shortage of car space and the passenger steamers frequently duplicated the car ferry sailings. The Company's third car ferry, the *Mona's Queen* [5], was named at the Ailsa yard at Troon on 21st December 1971. She became the first passenger motor ship in the Manx fleet and also the first to be fitted with a bow-thrust unit which greatly assisted in speeding up berthing times.

The *Peveril* [3] was converted to a container ship by her builders in early 1972. Her cargo handling cranes were removed and a cellular system for 56 twenty-foot equivalent units (TEUs) was installed. The weekly Ramsey freight sailing was withdrawn and the cargo vessel *Ramsey*, which had made her maiden voyage

*The **Mona's Isle** (5) berthing at Queen's Pier, Ramsey en route from Belfast to Douglas.* (Stan Basnett)

*The **Manx Maid** (2) carrying the second version of the Company logo which was adopted during 1984.* (Ian Collard)

175

*The Company's first diesel-powered passenger/ car ferry was the **Mona's Queen** (5) which was built by Ailsa at Troon in 1972. (Ferry Publications Library)*

as recently as February 1965, was effectively redundant as was the *Fenella* of 1951.

The entry into service of the *Mona's Queen* meant that for the first time continuous car ferry working could be maintained during the winter months. Until the 1971-1972 winter, the *Manxman* had been pressed into stints of winter service whilst the *Manx Maid* and *Ben-my-Chree* received their annual overhauls.

As a 'running-mate' for the *Peveril*, the Steam Packet Company chartered the *Spaniel* from the Belfast Steamship Company in 1973 and then bought her outright in November and renamed her *Conister* [2]. The Ailsa Company at Troon converted her to Steam Packet requirements and she was equipped to carry 46 TEUs.

The replacement of the old Liverpool Landing Stage became a priority in 1973. A new and much smaller stage was planned but in the inflationary 1970s the cost of this was spiralling out of control and reached an estimated £1.25 million by the end of 1973.

Over the winter months of 1973/1974, the price of fuel oil quadrupled and the Company was forced to increase the passenger return fare by a massive 36% to £9 with effect from February 1974. The *Mona's Queen* introduced car ferry sailings to Dublin later in the year.

On Bank Holiday Monday 26th August 1974 there were seven Steam Packet passenger vessels berthed together in Douglas

*The **King Orry** (4) was disposed of in November 1975 and towed to Glasson Dock for breaking. However, during a gale in the following January the ship broke free from her moorings and stranded herself at the top of the tide on a nearby mud bank. (Liverpool Maritime Museum)*

*The **Lady of Mann** (2) was the Company's fourth and final side-loader. She is seen on the stocks at Troon shortly before her launch in December 1975. (Bruce Peter collection)*

The **Lady of Mann** (2) in pristine condition when new. During the ship's career a number of major modifications have taken place to her basic layout.
(Bruce Peter collection)

Harbour which would never happen again as the *Tynwald* was sold later in the year. It was also announced that there would be no Heysham - Douglas sailings in 1975 as there was 'insufficient passenger potential to meet the additional operating costs.'

The *Manx Maid* struck the Fort Anne Jetty at Douglas whilst attempting to berth in bad weather on 13th November 1974, and three weeks later the northern section of the old Landing Stage at Liverpool sank, taking with it the Company's booking office.

The *Manx Maid* was trapped in a Birkenhead dry dock until the end of May 1975. A prolonged industrial dispute had broken out at Cammell Laird which meant finding alternative overhaul arrangements for the rest of the fleet.

However, the 1975 summer season turned out to be very successful for the Steam Packet Company. With fine and sunny weather predominating, the Company carried a total of 909,556 passengers, the highest figure for very many years and a total which has not been exceeded since, nor is ever likely to be. At the end of the summer the *King Orry* made her final crossings on 31st August. She had made 7,412 sailings for the Company in the course of a remarkable thirty-year career, and had steamed 516,770 miles and carried 3,325,500 passengers.

The Company's fourth car ferry, the *Lady of Mann* [2] was launched from the Troon yard of the Ailsa Shipbuilding Company on 4th December 1975. For the first time, the car ferries outnumbered the classic passenger steamers in the fleet. The new 'Lady' arrived at Douglas on 29th June 1976, several weeks late. She had missed the T.T. Race traffic which the Company carried with just six vessels. The new ship was a more powerful vessel

than her elder sister, the *Mona's Queen*, and did not suffer the teething troubles of the earlier vessel.

Car ferry sailings from Fleetwood were inaugurated in 1976 but the response was less than enthusiastic as only 2,000 cars were conveyed on 88 sailings, an average of just 22 per crossing. Despite the summer of 1976 being the hottest of the twentieth century, the Company reported a drop of 12,000 passengers when compared to 1975.

In mid-January 1977 the Chairman of the Isle of Man Harbour Board announced that roll on - roll off facilities were being considered by his Board, but their provision depended on two major factors: 1] the building of a breakwater extension likely to cost around £5 million, and 2] the provision of a linkspan which might require another £2 million. Notwithstanding this statement, the Isle of Man Government later in 1977 agreed to expenditure of £650,000 to support the setting-up of a ro-ro service by a group of Manx businessmen which would operate in direct competition with the Steam Packet Company. This sum would cover approximately half the cost of a linkspan installation in Douglas Harbour.

In 1977 the Company's operating costs were higher than expected; for instance the annual fuel bill amounted to £1,270,000, six times the 1973 figure. With the threat of a new operator commencing on Isle of Man routes in 1978 it was decided to reduce the Steam Packet fleet to six ships and the *Snaefell* was offered for sale. The Steam Packet Directors made an exploratory trip from London to Zeebrugge and back on the Boeing Jetfoil operated by P&O to assess its potential for Manx routes.

CHAPTER NINE

Manx Line and the Merger 1978 – 1986

1978: Island's first multi-storey car park at Douglas opened

1979: Margaret Thatcher became first woman U.K. Prime Minister, 3rd May

1979: Queen Elizabeth II and Prince Philip attended Millennium Tynwald ceremony

1982: Argentina invaded the Falkland Islands, 2nd April

1983: New U.K. £1 coin introduced, 21st April

1983: Princess Alexandra opened the new breakwater at Douglas (£10.5 million) followed by the billion gallon Sulby Reservoir

1984: Miners' strike against pit closures commenced 12th March

1984: IRA bomb at Grand Hotel, Brighton during Conservative Party Conference

1986: Major accident at Chernobyl nuclear power plant, USSR, 26th April

The Manx Line was formed in 1978 by a group of Island businessmen with the intention of providing roll on - roll off services to the Isle of Man. All the Steam Packet Company's car ferries had been specially built to load and unload from existing harbour facilities at Douglas, a system which had limited the size of vehicles carried to cars and light vans. By using Heysham as its U.K. port with its existing loading ramp and a new linkspan at Douglas, Manx Line would overcome this problem.

On 23rd March 1978 the 2,753 ton motor vessel *Monte Castillo* of Bilbao arrived at Douglas and carried out berthing trials. The former Aznar Line vessel then sailed for Leith for a complete refit. Manx Line advertised its new Heysham to Douglas service as commencing on 1st June. The new company was accepting bookings up to late May when it suddenly announced that the new service would not be running before 1st July. Owing to industrial strife the *Monte Castillo* (now renamed *Manx Viking*) did not leave Leith until 29th July, arriving in Douglas on 31st July.

*The **Ben-my-Chree** (5) and the Thoresen ferry **Viking III** at Douglas in Spring 1980. The modern drive-through car ferry was on charter to rival company Manx Line.* (Stan Basnett)

The Steam Packet Company had to arrange extra sailings to carry the Manx Line T.T. traffic during the first ten days of June. After further delays the *Manx Viking* made her inaugural crossing from Heysham to Douglas on 26th August 1978. On 8th September, only a fortnight after the service started, one of her diesel engines broke a piston and sailings were again suspended. With the enormous loss of revenue as a result of starting the service so late in the season, plus the high cost of work carried out at Leith and Heysham, Manx Line was rapidly running into serious financial trouble. On 20th October came the announcement that Sealink and James Fisher had taken over the company.

On the night of 1st December 1978, in the first severe easterly gale which had occurred since the installation of the Manx Line Victoria Pier linkspan, it broke adrift and severed its connection with the approach road. Just under two years earlier, in January 1977, the Harbour Board Chairman had said that a prerequisite for siting a linkspan in Douglas Harbour was the construction of an extension to the Battery Pier breakwater to protect the harbour from easterly gales. In its haste to assist the new Manx Line this advice had been ignored by the Government and the result was plain for all to see on the morning of 2nd December.

Without the linkspan facility the *Manx Viking* was unable to operate and was despatched for major overhaul at the Belfast yard of Harland & Wolff on 12th December. There were many on the Isle of Man who considered the Manx Line operation finished.

The run of easterly gales continued throughout the winter of 1978 - 1979 and the Steam Packet Company diverted its vessel to Peel on eighteen occasions - three times the normal winter average. In November 1979 the Isle of Man Government finally 'grasped the nettle' and approved the expenditure of £7.2 million to protect and extend the Battery Pier at Douglas.

The *Manx Viking* was back on the Heysham - Douglas service in May 1979 using a temporary structure incorporating a Bailey bridge erected on the north side of the King Edward VIII Pier at Douglas. The replacement linkspan finally arrived and was in place on the Victoria Pier in July when the full ro-ro Manx Line service was restored.

*Storm-force 11 winds lash the Island as the **Manxman** passes the end of the Battery Pier and heads for Liverpool in November 1965.* (Frank Hodson)

Monday 30th June 1980 was the 150th anniversary of the launch of the Isle of Man Steam Packet Company's first vessel, the paddle steamer *Mona's Isle* [1]. Accordingly the *Mona's Isle* [5] was rostered to take a 'Round the Island' excursion to mark the occasion. Due to increased operating costs the Company could no longer keep a reserve of vessels for summer-only use and so the 'Isle' was offered for sale at the end of the season. The Liverpool to Llandudno excursion sailings ceased with her passing.

In September 1980 the Steam Packet Company announced that it had placed a contract for the construction of a linkspan with O.Y. Navire AB of Finland. The linkspan was towed into Douglas on 2nd June 1981 and was ballasted into position on the south Edward Pier. To operate a new roll on - roll off freight service the Company had chartered the *NF Jaguar* from P&O. The ro-ro service was inaugurated on 19th June and the *Peveril* [3] and the *Conister* [2] were immediately made redundant.

1981 proved to be the Steam Packet's worst year of trading in its long history. After three very good summers, the number of staying visitors to the Isle of Man conveyed by the Company fell by 21.5% and the number of day-excursionists was down by 39%.

The *Manxman* [2] was retained in the fleet for the 1982 season. She was now the very last 'classic' passenger steamer operating in British waters. However, in the generally depressed state of affairs it became clear that it was no longer economically possible to retain her and she was offered for sale at the end of the season, at which time the Llandudno - Douglas sailings would also cease. The *Manxman* was bought for static use at Preston and she sailed from Liverpool under her own steam on 3rd October carrying 1,000 passengers bound for Preston. At 12.48 she was alongside in the Albert Edward Dock - finally 'Finished with Engines' after 27 years.

The high charter fees for the *NF Jaguar* were a major factor in the Steam Packet's freight service not being viable. Consequently, towards the end of 1982 the Company exercised its option to purchase the vessel. The vessel was painted in Steam Packet colours and renamed *Peveril* [4].

*The **Manx Maid** off the Liverpool Landing Stage with the Cheshire bank of the Mersey in the distance.* (Ian Collard)

It was becoming evident in 1982 that the Manx tourist industry was in rapid decline. Equally evident was the fact that there was just not room for two passenger ship operators on Isle of Man routes. The Steam Packet Company returned to profitability in 1983 after the two loss-making years of 1981 and 1982. Tenders were received for a new multi-purpose ro-ro vessel, but the lowest price quoted exceeded £20 million.

The *Peveril's* cargo sailings in 1984 were constantly disrupted by strikes and the Company's major freight clients transferred to Sealink/Manx Line. The *Peveril* had the capacity to carry all the cargo requirements of the Isle of Man but in reality was now carrying only 50% of that cargo.

The U.K. Government sold Sealink (of which Manx Line was a part) to Sea Containers Limited of Bermuda on 27th July 1984. Thus commenced James Sherwood's involvement in the Manx shipping scene.

At the end of another dismal summer season the steam turbine car ferries *Manx Maid* and *Ben-my-Chree* were offered for sale despite there being considerable useful life left in both of them. A 30% increase in the price of the heavy grade of fuel oil used by the steamers had rendered them totally uneconomic.

On 19th October 1984 the Steam Packet Company purchased the ro-ro vessel *Tamira*, formerly Townsend Thoresen's *Free Enterprise III*. The vessel was lying at Valletta, Malta and Captain Vernon Kinley and a Manx crew flew out to Malta to bring her back to the Clyde. The Company signed an agreement with Burness, Corlett Limited, Naval Architects of Ramsey, in respect of professional advice for refurbishing the ship, which by now was renamed *Mona's Isle* [6].

*The former Spanish ferry **Monte Castillo** was acquired by the rival Manx Line and renamed **Manx Viking**. She started a rival service between Douglas and Heysham and began a period of fierce competition leading to an eventual merger with the Steam Packet in 1985. The vessel is seen leaving Douglas in Steam Packet colours. (Stan Basnett)*

The Company recorded a loss of £245,244 for 1984, and the year 1985 opened with a veil of secrecy hanging over future operations. No sailing schedules were published and no bookings were accepted for after 31st March. It was obvious that the Steam Packet Company was in severe financial difficulties.

At 09.30 on the morning of 1st February 1985 a press conference was hastily arranged at Imperial Buildings, the Company's head office at Douglas. A joint communiqué was issued from Sealink and the Steam Packet Company outlining a merger of their respective operations, the end of the Liverpool

*The **Mona's Isle** (6) was the shortest-lived of all Steam Packet vessels. Built as the **Free Enterprise III** for Townsend's Dover - Calais route in 1966, she came to the Island in April 1985 and remained for exactly six months. (John Clarkson collection)*

*In Autumn 1982, the **Manxman** (2) was purchased by a Preston-based company for use as a night-club. In early October, Captain Peter Corrin took her on a final public sailing from Liverpool to Preston Dock where she is seen on her arrival. The ship's 23 year fall from grace is well documented but there are ambitious plans to restore her to a berth at Birkenhead. (John Clarkson)*

*Following the disastrous 1985 season with the **Mona's Isle** (6), Sealink chartered to the Steam Packet their Stranraer - Larne ferry **Antrim Princess** which became the **Tynwald** (6) until her disposal in 1990. The **Mona's Queen** completes the picture. (Ferry Publications Library)*

*The roll on - roll off freight vessel **NF Jaguar** was chartered from P&O Ferries in the 1981 season and in the following year James Fisher of Barrow purchased her and chartered the vessel to the Steam Packet. She subsequently became the **Peveril** (4). (Ferry Publications Library)*

*The **Tynwald** (6) was built on the Tyne in 1967 becoming British Rail's first diesel-powered drive-through ferry.* (IOMSP Co Ltd)

service and the concentration of the main year-round service on Heysham from 1st April. The emotion of Steam Packet shareholders boiled over at a prolonged Extraordinary General Meeting held on 29th March which eventually approved the proposals for the merger.

On the eve of the merger, 31st March 1985, the situation was far from being auspicious. The Steam Packet's new flagship *Mona's Isle* was still at Govan with problems with her fire sprinkler system; the *Peveril* was strikebound at Liverpool; Sealink's *Antrim Princess* was not available to assist, and the *Manx Viking's* survey certificates were due to expire within 24 hours. The Heysham linkspan was blocked by the striking crew of the *Stena Sailor*.

A basic service was operated by the side-loaders *Mona's Queen* and *Lady of Mann*. More trouble was to follow when the *Mona's Isle* arrived in Douglas on 3rd April only to find that she would

*On board the **Tynwald** (6) in the main bar.* (IOMSP Co Ltd)

not fit either of the two linkspans. A fortnight later the Company announced that the ship had serious deadweight problems and could not carry anything like the loadings expected of her. Due to the extensive new passenger accommodation added, the usable cargo deadweight amounted to just 247 tonnes. Compare this to the 2,220 tons deadweight capacity on the present *Ben-my-Chree*! An inadequate bow-thrust unit meant that the 'Isle' was unmanageable in anything more than a moderate breeze and tugs were required both at Douglas and Heysham to assist in berthing.

The Company had to make arrangements to charter back the *Ben-my-Chree* (5) from her new owners to cover the T.T. period from 25th May until 9th June 1985 and she was re-registered in Liverpool for this period.

The Steam Packet Company Board meeting of 15th August resolved a number of outstanding problems. The *Mona's Isle* would be permanently withdrawn on 5th October after just six months with the Company and would be replaced by Sealink's *Antrim Princess*. The Board would take legal action in respect of the consultancy advice received about the *Mona's Isle*.

The *Antrim Princess* was renamed *Tynwald* [6] and by the end of 1985 her port of registry had been changed from Stranraer to Douglas. Between 1979 and 1985 the holiday seasonal arrivals in the Isle of Man had fallen from 634,616 to 351,240: a decrease of 45%.

In 1986 the Ardrossan sailings were transferred to a weekly seasonal service from Stranraer. A limited Liverpool summer service was introduced on Tuesdays and Saturdays using the *Lady of Mann*. The *Mona's Isle* was sold for £710,502 and was renamed *Al Fahad* for trading in the Red Sea.

The *Manx Viking* was withdrawn from service on 29th September 1986 to be replaced by the *Peveril*. Strike action over manning levels on the *Peveril* led to 58 sailings being lost on four separate occasions, followed by a strike from 4th - 11th December: the longest disruption to services by strikes since 1966.

CHAPTER TEN

Recent Times, the Take-over and the Sale 1987 – 2005

1987: Herald of Free Enterprise capsized off Zeebrugge, 193 dead, 6th March

1988: Terrorist bomb caused PanAm jumbo jet to crash on Lockerbie, 21st December

1989: Demolition of Berlin Wall commenced, 9th November

1990: Nelson Mandela freed from captivity, 11th February

1991: 'Operation Desert Storm' to liberate Kuwait from Iraqi troops, 17th January

1994: The Queen officially opened the Channel Tunnel, 6th May

1997: Hong Kong handed over to Chinese rule, 1st July

1998: Tynwald agreed that IOM should have an electricity cable link with UK

2001: Terrorist attack on World Trade Centre, New York, 11th September

2002: Queen Elizabeth The Queen Mother died at Easter, aged 101

2003: American and coalition attack against Iraq commenced, 20th March

A return to happier Steam Packet days took place in 1987 when the *Mona's Queen* operated a Heysham - Peel - Heysham charter on 4th July. In perfect weather and with 1,600 passengers on board, Captain Jack Ronan sailed the 'Queen' outwards to Peel via Langness and the Calf of Man, and returned to Heysham via the Point of Ayre and Maughold Head.

The crew of the *Tynwald* went on indefinite strike on Tuesday 29th December 1987 over the Company's proposals for revised pay and conditions. The *Tynwald* was at the Heysham linkspan at the outset of the strike and loaded vehicles were trapped on board for 47 days until the industrial action was called off on 13th February 1988.

The *Tynwald* was again off service due to illegal secondary strike action by her crew from 29th April until 14th May 1988. In order to safeguard the T.T. Race Week traffic, the Manx Government chartered the Skagerrak ferry *Bolette* from Fred. Olsen Lines at a cost of £1 million for three weeks.

At the end of 1988 the Isle of Man Government resolved to dispose of its stockholding in the Steam Packet Company and to compulsorily acquire the two Steam Packet-owned linkspans in Douglas Harbour.

*The **Mona's Queen** was chartered by La Poste in September 1989. She is seen entering Portsmouth Harbour with the **Pride of Le Havre** outward bound from the port. (John Hendy)*

*The **Manx Maid** (2) in the final stages of demolition at Garston in 1986. (John Clarkson collection)*

During the early months of 1989 the *Lady of Mann* was given a £2.6 million renovation and an increase in her car capacity at Birkenhead, she returned to service on 26th May with a passenger certificate for just 1,000 (she was licensed to carry 1,600 on her entry into service in 1976).

The *Peveril*'s starboard variable pitch propeller mechanism jammed in the reverse position as she was moving astern to the 'Navire' linkspan at Douglas on 14th July 1989. Extensive damage was caused to the linkspan necessitating it being towed to Birkenhead for repairs. Both the *Peveril* and the *Tynwald* had to use the 'MacGregor' linkspan on the Victoria Pier, resulting in much congestion at the height of the summer season.

After being laid up at Birkenhead for over four years the Company's last steamer, the *Ben-my-Chree* of 1966, left for breaking up at Santander on 16th August.

Severe weather at the end of 1989 resulted in all sailings being cancelled on Christmas Eve. For the first time since before the war, daylight crossings were operated on Christmas Day with the *Tynwald* making a return trip to Heysham.

On 7th February 1990 the Steam Packet Company obtained permission from its shareholders to purchase the multi-purpose vessel *Channel Entente* (ex *Saint Eloi*) which had been built in 1972 for the train ferry service from Dover to Dunkirk. Captain Edward Fargher and a Steam Packet crew brought the *Channel Entente* round from Dunkirk in early January 1990 and after testing both the linkspans in Douglas Harbour, berthing trials were carried out at all ports used by the Company. After the *Mona's Isle* episode, they were taking no chances!

With the advent of the *Channel Entente*, the *Tynwald* was redundant and she was returned to Sealink after her final Steam Packet sailings on 19th February. The new ship sailed from Douglas to Heysham on her maiden Steam Packet voyage on the afternoon of 19th February, having been delayed for nearly four

hours by bad weather. In extremely stormy conditions she immediately proved herself to be a good sea boat, in contrast to the very lively *Tynwald*.

The future ownership of the Company was put in doubt by a takeover bid launched in June 1990 on behalf of Sea Containers, who already owned 41% of the share capital. The bid of £1.15p per share was deemed wholly inadequate and on 2nd August Sea Containers withdrew its bid.

The extra vehicle capacity on the *Channel Entente* and the recently rebuilt *Lady of Mann* made the *Mona's Queen* redundant and she made her final sailing on 3rd September. The *Channel Entente* was given a major refit at Birkenhead in Autumn 1990. After returning to Douglas on 6th December she was renamed *King Orry* [5].

A limited Liverpool and Douglas winter service resumed in January 1991 on Saturdays only after a five-year gap and the new service rapidly gained popularity, carrying capacity loads most Saturdays. The Steam Packet Company was recovering from the doldrums of the 1980s, and in 1992 pre-tax profits were up on the previous year to £4.1 million.

Whilst taking the 18.15 sailing from Liverpool to Douglas on 14th November the *King Orry* suffered a steering failure in the Queen's Channel in the Mersey approaches and grounded on Taylor's Bank. Hoylake lifeboat and two tugs went to the scene and the 'Orry' was refloated on the rising tide at 22.30. She was towed back to Liverpool where her 374 passengers were transferred to the Adelphi Hotel. The *Lady of Mann* was immediately brought out of dock and restored the sailings the following day.

In Spring 1993 the Steam Packet Company announced 'with regret' that it had been unable to agree terms with Sea Containers for the charter of a SeaCat for the summer season.

On 2nd June 1993, at the height of the T.T. race traffic, the

Lady of Mann was manoeuvring in Douglas harbour on arrival from Liverpool, but instead of going astern into No.4 berth on the Victoria Pier she surged ahead and collided with the Battery Pier. A vast backlog of traffic built up and Caledonian MacBrayne's *Pioneer* operated a Gourock to Douglas sailing while the *SeaCat Scotland* made one return trip to Douglas from Stranraer. The 'Lady' was back in service, with a temporary passenger certificate, on 4th June.

In March 1994 came the surprise news that a SeaCat was to be operated on Manx routes for the summer season and that the *Lady of Mann* would be laid up. At the Company's A.G.M. on 5th May the shareholders expressed their concern and demanded assurances that the Directors were confident of the success of the venture. The events of a decade earlier were uncomfortably fresh in the memories of many shareholders!

The T.T. race traffic in 1994 was carried by the *King Orry*, the *Lady of Mann* and the freight vessel *Peveril*. On 28th June the *Lady of Mann* was laid up at Birkenhead and on that same day the *SeaCat Isle of Man*, on charter from Sea Containers, made her inaugural crossing from Douglas to Fleetwood, taking just 94 minutes for the passage. The following day the SeaCat sailed from Douglas to Liverpool in 2 hours 20 minutes. A £350,000 pontoon and ramp were provided at Liverpool to accommodate the craft.

A long spell of calm and settled weather prevailed in July and August 1994 and it was not until 28th August that gales disrupted the SeaCat schedule. The fast craft was not permitted to sail in

waves exceeding 3.5 metres in height. In August 1994 work started on the installation of the Manx Government's own linkspan on the north side of the Edward Pier at Douglas.

During her winter overhaul of 1994/95, the *King Orry* was transferred from the Bahamas register to the Manx register while in May the new Manx Government linkspan arrived from Holland and was lifted into position at the north Edward Pier at Douglas by the floating crane *Mersey Mammoth*.

The problem of how to employ the *Lady of Mann* was solved in the summer of 1995 by chartering her to the Porto Santo Line of Madeira. After operating the T.T. schedules for eighteen days, the 'Lady' was laid up until 17th July when she left Birkenhead on the four-day passage to Funchal, Madeira.

On 11th July the Manx Government finally approved the ten-year 'User Agreement' for its new linkspan. The Agreement required the Steam Packet Company to operate each year a minimum of 486 return passenger services to north-west England / North Wales, of which at least 104 must be to a port in the Liverpool / Holyhead range. At least 63 return services were required to Irish ports. Freight services had to be provided for a minimum of five days per week, with a limited service on the sixth. There had to be a minimum investment in ships, and fare increases had to be pegged to the Manx rate of inflation. In return the Steam Packet Company received sole user rights to the new linkspan.

On 27th September, the *SeaCat Isle of Man* was struck by what

*The **Saint Eloi** was originally built for the Dover-Dunkirk train ferry service. She is seen here outward bound from Dover to Dunkirk in 1986. (Miles Cowsill)*

*Following agreement for the Company to purchase the **Channel Entente** (ex **Saint Eloi**), the vessel operated under this name for her first season prior to her major overhaul and refit in 1990 before becoming the **King Orry** (5). (IOMSP Co Ltd)*

was described as a 'freak wave' near the Mersey Bar. The craft sustained some structural damage and the watertight bow visor was twisted. The SeaCat was sent to Cammell Laird for repairs and an official investigation was immediately ordered. The Company warned that, due to her £6,000 a day charter fee, it expected a drop in profits for 1995.

On 30th October 1995 the Steam Packet Directors decided to dispense with the fast craft in 1996. The *Lady of Mann* returned from her Madeira charter in November and the *Mona's Queen* was sold to new owners in the Philippines. The 1995 results showed pre-tax profits down by £4 million to just £458,000. Half of this was due to the high cost of operating the SeaCat.

On 29th March 1996 it was announced that the Isle of Man Steam Packet Company had lost its independence after 166 years of operation and that Sea Containers Isle of Man now owned 58% of the shares. Subsequently most remaining shareholders accepted Sea Containers' offer and by the date of the 166th and final Annual General Meeting of the Members of the Company on 2nd May, Sea Containers controlled over 95% of the shares and the Company was delisted on the Stock Exchange. With no fast craft in operation in 1996, it was left to the *King Orry* and the *Lady of Mann* to provide the passenger services.

In early 1997 it was announced that an order had been placed with Van der Giessen-de Noord of Rotterdam for a new ro-pax vessel to replace the *King Orry* and the *Peveril*. At 125 metres in length the new vessel would be built to the near maximum dimensions for using the harbours at Heysham and Douglas.

The *SeaCat Isle of Man* returned to Manx waters on 21st May 1997. Her programme of sailings was far more intensive than in 1994 and 1995. Following the T.T. traffic sailings, the *Lady of*

*This interesting view shows **SeaCat Isle of Man** passing close to the Chicken Rock Lighthouse on the occasion of her first round-the-Island trip for the Company. (IOMSP Co Ltd)*

King Orry (5)

Top left: *Cafeteria.*

Top right : *Side Lounge.*

Above: *Drivers' Lounge Area.*

Left: *Aft Bar*

Below: *The **King Orry** undergoing her major refit in 1990.*

(Miles Cowsill/IOMSP Co Ltd)

This outstanding view shows the newly-painted and refurbished ***King Orry*** *(5) outward bound from Douglas to Heysham in 1991.* (IOMSP Co Ltd)

*The former Caledonian MacBrayne vessel **Claymore** is pictured arriving with a full load of bikers during the TT season inward bound from Heysham.* (IOMSP Co Ltd)

Mann opened a new Liverpool - Dublin service on 12th June, providing a scheduled six-and-a-half hour passage. Given favourable tides, the 'Lady' often completed the passage in well under six hours.

The keel of the new ro-pax vessel, to be named *Ben-my-Chree* [6], was laid on 28th October 1997. At this early stage concerns began to be voiced about her limited passenger certificate for just 500 passengers.

The *SeaCat Isle of Man* was replaced by *SeaCat Danmark* for the 1998 summer season and she entered service on 21st May. During the 1998 T.T. race period, the *Lady of Mann* operated her usual busy schedule and on 17th June she sailed for the Azores on a three-month bareboat charter, sailing between eight ports within the group of islands.

The Liverpool - Dublin service, operated by the 'Lady' in 1997, was taken over by the monohull fast craft *SuperSeaCat Two* in 1998. The new craft, restricted to sailing in seas of under three metres in height, had a very mixed summer and suffered from recurrent technical problems as well as bad weather cancellations. The *Lady of Mann*, back from her charter to the Azores, covered as many of the cancelled services as was possible.

The new £24 million Steam Packet ro-pax vessel *Ben-my-Chree* arrived in Douglas from her builders on 6th July 1998. She entered service in 'freight mode' when the ro-ro freight vessel

*The **Lady of Mann** (2) is seen on summer charter in Madeira.* (IOMSP Co Ltd)

The **King Orry** (5) leaving Douglas in her final Steam Packet livery. (Miles Cowsill)

Peveril was withdrawn from service and laid up at Birkenhead.

The 'Ben' entered full passenger service on 4th August 1998 and to enable the new vessel to settle in, the Steam Packet kept the *King Orry* in service as back-up vessel until 29th September, after which she was laid up at Birkenhead. The 'Orry' was quickly sold for £2 million to Fion s.p.a. of Italy and left the Mersey for the last time on 23rd October carrying the name *Moby Love*, registered in Naples, but still in full Steam Packet livery.

In October 1998 the Manx Parliament appointed a Select Committee on the Isle of Man Steam Packet Company with a remit to look at the frequency and quality of passenger services following criticism of the new *Ben-my-Chree*. A couple of months

later the Company announced that the 'Ben' would not in future carry more than 350 passengers per sailing, which was considered a 'comfort level'.

For the summer seasonal fast craft services, the *SeaCat Isle of Man* returned to Manx waters, commencing her sailings on 31st March 1999. The *Lady of Mann* returned to Douglas on 26th May with 900 passengers on a day excursion from Llandudno, and the next day brought in 600 trippers from Fleetwood. These early season day cruises have been a popular feature of the 'Lady's' programme since they were introduced in 1997.

Following the T.T. period, the *Lady of Mann* retired to dock until 23rd July. Rather than go on charter to the sunnier climes of

The launch of the **Ben-my-Chree** (6) at the Dutch yard of Van der Giessen-de Noord. (Ferry Publications Library)

Mrs Joan Gelling with the then Bishop of Sodor and Man, the Rt. Rev'd Noel Jones who blessed the ship prior to her launch. (Ferry Publications Library)

The **Ben-my-Chree** (6) manoeuvres slowly up the New Waterway in Rotterdam prior to undertaking sea trials. (Ferry Publications Library)

The **Ben-my-Chree** (6) is seen following completion of her sea trials off the Hook of Holland prior to being delivered to the Company. (Ferry Publications Library)

The former **King Orry** (6) was sold by the Isle of Man Steam Packet Company to Moby Line of Italy. She is seen here as the **Moby Love** at the port of Portoferraio. (Richard Seville)

The **Mona's Queen** was acquired by a Philippine company MBRS Lines in 1995 and renamed **Mary the Queen**. She is seen here operating in the Philippines showing every sign of a former Steam Packet vessel. (Ray Smith)

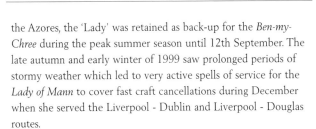

the Azores, the 'Lady' was retained as back-up for the *Ben-my-Chree* during the peak summer season until 12th September. The late autumn and early winter of 1999 saw prolonged periods of stormy weather which led to very active spells of service for the *Lady of Mann* to cover fast craft cancellations during December when she served the Liverpool - Dublin and Liverpool - Douglas routes.

The Steam Packet's 2000 summer season got into full swing with the T.T. motor cycle traffic at the end of May and six vessels were used: the *Ben-my-Chree*, the *Lady of Mann*, the *SuperSeaCat Two* and 'Three' and the *SeaCat Isle of Man* and 'Scotland'. Following the T.T. traffic the *Lady of Mann* sailed to the Azores for another three months on charter.

Following two difficult winters, the *Lady of Mann* was scheduled to provide the Liverpool - Douglas winter service from early November 2000 until the end of February 2001.

The 25-year-old *Lady of Mann* entered Cammell Laird's Birkenhead yard at the end of February 2001 for work to start on her refit and SOLAS upgrading. The most visible feature is the new high-speed rescue craft fitted to her starboard side boat deck.

The year 2001 was dominated in the United Kingdom by the outbreak of foot and mouth disease. The Manx Government took the decision to cancel the annual T.T. motor cycle races as part of the precautions to try and prevent the disease reaching the Isle of Man. The Steam Packet normally carries over 35,000 passengers, 15,000 motorcycles and 3,500 other vehicles in connection with

The **Tynwald** (6) was replaced by the **Channel Entente** in 1990. She was in service until 2003 as the **Giuseppe D' Abundo** operating for Medmar; her future is now uncertain at the grand age of 38 years old. She is pictured here as the **Lauro Express**. (John May)

*The **Ben-my-Chree** (6) is captured here in the evening sun arriving from Heysham showing the addition to her passenger accommodation in 2004. (Miles Cowsill)*

Ben-my-Chree (6)

Top: *The **Ben-my-Chree** swings in the narrow confines of Heysham harbour following her arrival from Douglas.*

Middle Row Left: *The new forward 1st Lounge was provided on the **Ben-my-Chree** during her refit in 2004.*

Above Left: *The main passenger and Promenade Cafeteria area on board the **Ben-my-Chree**.*

Middle Row Right: *A new after Quiet Lounge was provided in 2003.*

Above Right: *The new Triskele Bar area provided during the 2004 refit.*

(All photos Miles Cowsill)

The **Lady of Mann** (2) at Cammell Laird shipyard in Birkenhead showing the external alterations which were undertaken to comply with the latest SOLAS requirements. (IOMSP Co)

the races. The *Lady of Mann*'s Irish Sea schedule was cancelled completely, but she was away to the Azores yet again on her annual three-month charter to Acor Line.

In early 2002 the Steam Packet Company agreed a five-year extension to the 'User Agreement' with the Manx Government concerning the linkspan on the north Edward Pier at Douglas.

Following the cancellation of the T.T. races in 2001, there had been some uncertainty as to how well the event would be supported in 2002. However, the final outcome, according to Manx Tourism Minister David Cretney, was "the highest recorded figure for T.T. ferry traffic for at least 20 years". The intensive schedules worked during the T.T. period allow little flexibility if

The **Lady of Mann** (2) makes a magnificent view inward bound sailing light to Douglas from Heysham in June 2004. (Miles Cowsill)

*This interesting view during the TT period of 2004 shows the **Ben-my-Chree** (6) and **Lady of Mann** (2) loading for their evening sailings to Heysham with the **Rapide** having just arrived from Belfast.* (Miles Cowsill)

things go wrong, and the *Ben-my-Chree* had to be withdrawn for emergency repairs on 28th / 29th May during which time the *Lady of Mann* provided extra sailings.

On 24th March 2003, Sea Containers announced that it had put the Isle of Man Steam Packet Company up for sale with a price tag of £150 million. The Manx Government immediately indicated that it was not interested in buying or putting money into the Company.

During its association with the Isle of Man, dating back to the 1985 merger with Manx Line, Sea Containers introduced the ro-pax vessel *Ben-my-Chree* and successfully weathered the storm of protest caused by her passenger accommodation. Sea Containers also pioneered the use of large fast craft in Manx waters.

The new owners of the Isle of Man Steam Packet Company were Montagu Private Equity who purchased the Company from Sea Containers for £142 million. The deal was effective from 30th

*The evening sun captures the **Ben-my-Chree** (6) coming astern at the King Edward Pier inward bound from Heysham. The Dutch-built ship has proved to be extremely reliable and is the main lifeline of the Company's year-round operations.* (Miles Cowsill)

The **SuperSeaCat Two** swings off the King Edward Pier on arrival from Liverpool during the 2004 T.T. season. (Miles Cowsill)

June 2003. Hamish Ross, the Steam Packet's Managing Director, commented: "We are delighted that Montagu have chosen to acquire the Steam Packet under its existing management team." Once again the Company was now very much its own master.

It was announced in December 2003 that additional passenger areas were to be built on the *Ben-my-Chree* at a cost of £1.5 million. The new accommodation allows the vessel to carry her full passenger complement of 500.

The *Ben-my-Chree* returned to service in early February 2004 following the extension to her accommodation aft which provided a new Quiet Lounge and bar. The existing reclining seating lounge forward was converted to make a new 1st Lounge to bring the vessel in tandem with the facilities offered by other ships in the Company's operations. During the major refit of the *Ben-my-Chree*, the *Lady of Mann* covered for her absence with the Swedish-owned ship *Hoburgen*.

The Isle of Man had a record T.T. season for 2004 and once again a variety of vessels supported the operations during the period, including the *SuperSeaCat Two* and the *Rapide*. Once again, the *Lady of Mann* went south to the Azores on her charter

and returned again to Irish Sea operations in late October. During the winter period there were no fast craft operations, leaving only the conventional vessels to maintain services to the Island. In spite of a very severe winter, the Company were able to maintain operations at most times. The *SeaCat Isle of Man* was put up for sale at the end of the season and was acquired during early 2005 by a new operator between Liverpool and Dublin, following the decision of the Isle of Man Steam Packet Company to withdraw from this route.

For the 175th anniversary year, the *SuperSeaCat Two* was earmarked to maintain fast ferry operations with the *Ben-my-Chree* maintaining the Heysham service again. It seems likely that the *Lady of Mann* will not see any further service to the Isle of Man after the T.T. period in 2005 as she will be disposed of to a new operator, after 29 years of valiant service for the Company. The vessel may return as part of the sale agreement to the Island for TT periods. The Company today serves a modern and very different Island from that of years ago. To do that well the Steam Packet Company fleet has been modernised to provide a mix of conventional and fast ferries to meet the needs of both the freight and passenger markets. The *Ben-my-Chree* has proved to be a great 'all rounder' providing good car and passenger capacity whilst delivering a first class service to the freight sector. She has enough freight capacity to meet the Island's needs well into the 21st century thus ensuring that the Isle of Man's economic development is in no way constrained by lack of shipping capacity. The fast ferry services are there to carry out the core passenger and car carrying duties at times of higher demand. They have transformed the passenger business, reversing the decline of a few years ago. The passenger and car market has grown by over 40% since 1996 aided by heavy investment of some £55m in a more modern fleet and by much more aggressive marketing of the Steam Packet services, especially in North West England. The Company continues to closely monitor fast ferry development with the eventual aim of replacing the *SuperSeaCat* with a bigger and faster fast ferry capable of year round operation. As the Isle of Man Steam Packet Company celebrates its 175th anniversary with great pride in its past it can look with confidence to a bright and exciting future.

The **SeaCat Isle of Man** operated her last season on the Irish Sea for the Steam Packet Company in 2004. She is seen here swinging off the berth outward bound to Liverpool. (Miles Cowsill)

The **Ben-my-Chree** (5) at Peel having been diverted from Douglas due to easterly gales which made Douglas untenable before the new breakwater was built. (Stan Basnett)

CHAPTER ELEVEN

The A to Z of Steam Packet Captains
Compiled by Captain Jack Ronan

It is with much humility, a sense of honour and a privilege that I have been chosen to make this tribute to my colleagues and I hope that I have given it due justice."

Preface

The Company's 1930 centenary record gives mention to and illustrates many of the Captains who served during its first one hundred years.

Since then much has been written concerning the Company and its ships but the human aspect has for too long been overlooked. The following chapter attempts to redress the balance and brings the story of the Manx seafarer and his traditions right up to date.

The 1904 Steam Packet book states, "One of the most potent causes of the success of the Company is the fact that it has always insisted on having First Class officers and men aboard its steamers. Each and every one of them was an excellent navigator and seaman, no Captain could have long retained his position if he had not been endowed with those capabilities."

Of the Company, the famous Manx poet and writer the Rev'd T.E. Brown wrote, "I think I knew all the old Captains of the Isle of Man Steam Packet Company's service – they were grand old fellows. They differed in point of ability, of temper, of social aptness and popular ways. But they were all of them men and gentlemen. It is remarkable that the service should have turned out a type of officer so uniformly courteous and efficient."

These potted biographies show that the majority of Steam Packet Captains came from the humblest of origins and their seagoing experiences started at a very early age. During their first four years they would gather experience that would prepare them for their first certificates which were more familiarly known as 'tickets.'

After obtaining a 'ticket,' life became one continual period of study until such time that the Master's examination was passed. Even then they would not be promoted to Captain until all the necessary pilotage certificates were also gained and these included Liverpool, Belfast, Morecambe Bay (Fleetwood and Heysham), Ardrossan and latterly Dublin. Thereafter the Captains were expected to keep abreast of the many and continuous changes.

Captain Jack Ronan

Promotion has always depended on the availability of positions. Until 1938 it was not unknown for Masters to continue their service into their seventies but the introduction of pension funds in that year changed this situation. Even so, some officers had to wait well into their fifties and complete over twenty years' service before gaining their ultimate goal.

Regrettably it has not been possible to include all ranks and departments in this manuscript. Time, space and other circumstances would not permit this. I would, however, dedicate much credit to my Engineer colleague Shipmates and especially their Superintendent Engineer Mike Casey whose contribution is greatly acknowledged. Originally this work was simply going to cover the post-1945 period which encompasses the writer's own time in service but thanks to many friends and their families (and here I must above all make mention of Cecil Mitchell) I have been able to go back even further. Every effort has been made to achieve total accuracy but no doubt

*The **Conister** (1) was the first rung on the promotion ladder and was where most Masters learnt the responsibility of Captaincy. She was scrapped in 1965. (Captain Jack Ronan collection)*

there will be errors and omissions.

Of immense value has been the discovery of the old Company Minute Books, which are now lodged with Manx National Heritage and much information has been gleaned from them. I must thank Roger Sims, the Librarian and Archivist for permitting the books to be viewed and for his kind and patient interest. Captain Tom Harrison must also be thanked for allowing me access to his wonderful collection of old photographs.

The men herein have always been held in the highest esteem by the people of the Island and further afield. They were men apart – a select band of brothers. They share a common bond in that they are both men of the sea and the Steam Packet – known today as 'Steamies.'

Today's Steam Packet is a far cry from that of yesteryear and it is unfair to compare them, but I feel confident when I write that the people of the Steam Packet are as courteous, competent and efficient as they ever were.

J.E. Ronan
Castletown
May 2005

List of Captains in their seniority 1935-2005

Publishers' Note: *Although for ease of reference we have placed the 72 Steam Packet Captains in alphabetical order, at Captain Ronan's suggestion we have also included the following list which gives them in chronological sequence and therefore according to seniority. In order that the lists can be cross-referenced, each Captain has been allocated a number based on the date that he was appointed to the position of Master by the Steam Packet Company.*

1	W. Cain	19	P.J. Bridson	37	A.W.G. Kissack	55	T.K. Crellin
2	W. Gawne	20	W. Squires	38	T.H. Corteen	56	R. Adams
3	H. Quine	21	O. Taylor	39	A. Clucas	57	P.C. Corrin
4	R. Clucas, Snr	22	J.F. Collister	40	H.N. Kinley	58	S.T. Cowin
5	J.J. Comish	23	G.R. Kinley	41	B.C. Corlett	59	J. Woods
6	A. Lee	24	W.H. Crellin	42	J.R. Kinley	60	A. Bridson
7	C.A. Kinley	25	E.Q. Farrington	43	H.E. Collister	61	G. Peters
8	W. Watson	26	T.L. Corkill	44	M. Maughan	62	C. Duggan
9	T. Quayle	27	J.H. Whiteway	45	J.S. Kennaugh	63	N. Wild
10	T.C. Woods	28	T.E. Cain	46	J.B. Quirk	64	R.J. Moore
11	G. Woods	29	J.H. Kerruish	47	C.H. Collister	65	A. Albiston
12	W. Qualtrough	30	J.E. Quirk	48	J.E. Ronan	66	M. Leadley
13	J.J. Keig	31	R. Clucas, Jnr	49	E.C. Fargher	67	D. O'Toole
14	R. Duggan	32	L. Callow	50	K. Bridson	68	J. Kelly
15	J.W. Cubbon	33	W.E. McMeiken	51	B.H. Moore	69	T.E. Harrison
16	P.B. Cowley	34	R.E. Gelling	52	R.M. Dickinson	70	S.M. Spenser
17	A. Holkham	35	F. Griffin	53	D.C. Hall	71	T.G. Moore
18	A. Whiteway	36	J.D. Craine	54	T.V. Kinley	72	D. Bell

Captain R. ADAMS (56)

Born in 1946 at Bromley in Kent, he spent two years at the London Nautical School before going to sea in 1962 as a cadet with Clan Line. During the next six years he met many Manx seamen which gave him the incentive to move to the Island where he chose Kirk Michael as his home. He joined the Steam Packet as a 2nd Officer in 1968 and became Chief Officer in 1971.

Master: 1978   First Command: *Conister* (2)

His first passenger command was the *Mona's Isle* (5) in 1978 after which he served on all the ships of that era but after the *Peveril's* charter to Belfast Freight Ferries he decided to join that company as Master of their *Saga Moon*.

Bob Adams fitted well into the Steam Packet routines during the period of his tenure and was a good and efficient seaman, a fine ship handler and made many friends who knew him as 'Bobsy.'

He later made his home in the Orkney Islands where he is presently a Marine Operations Manager at Scapa Flow controlling shipping movements, particularly those involved with the offshore oil industry.

175

Captain A. ALBISTON (65)

He was born in Stockport in 1953. Being half-Manx, he was educated for a while on the Island and during his later school years he served three summers with the Steam Packet in the *Ben-my-Chree* (5). On leaving school he joined the Bank Line as a cadet, rejoining the Steam Packet in 1978 as 2nd Officer. He obtained his Master's Foreign Going Certificate in 1983 becoming one of the few to have achieved this while working for the Steam Packet. He was in officer service for 19 years which was both a long time and a long wait by previous Company standards.

First Command: *SeaCat Isle of Man*

Thereafter he took command of both SeaCats and conventional vessels as required and in recent times has taken the *Lady of Mann* on charter to the Azores. Another young man who has proved his dedication to seafaring in general and the Steam Packet in particular in a most capable and competent manner. Alan Albiston was for some time 2nd Mate with the writer on the *Ben-my-Chree* (5) and proved a good shipmate.

Captain D. BELL (72)

Born on the south coast of England in 1968, he grew up in Yorkshire and at 13 went to the Trinity House Nautical School in Hull. He later joined the Royal Fleet Auxiliary as a deck cadet and was with the Armilla Patrol in the Persian Gulf during the Iran/ Iraq War of 1988, also serving in the Falklands. After achieving the rank of 2nd Officer he was 'released' in 1996 and joined the Steam Packet in that capacity on the *Peveril*.

After gaining his Master's Certificate, his first commands were the *SeaCat Isle of Man* and *Lady of Mann* in 2003. Dominic Bell is one of the more recent additions to our roll of honour and is an extremely competent and worthy successor to his predecessors illustrated in this chapter.

Captain A. BRIDSON (60)

He was born in Douglas in 1938 and went to the training ship *Vindicatrix* for training. Passing out successfully he joined the 'Pool' and sailed foreign-going out of Liverpool with various companies. In March 1957 he was in New Zealand where he saved the lives of two swimmers for which he was awarded the Royal Humane Society's Testimonial on Vellum.

He first joined the Steam Packet in 1956 on a seasonal basis as a seaman in the *Lady of Mann* (1), going 'foreign' each winter. After attending nautical college, he obtained his certificates and was promoted to 2nd Mate in 1967 and then Chief Officer in 1977.

Master: 1985   First Command: *Peveril* (4)

He served on all the ships of his age, the last being the *Ben-my-Chree* (6). Allan Bridson proved himself to be an excellent seaman and a fine ship Master and handler. He was always most popular with his colleagues and passengers alike. He retired in 2000 after a lifetime at sea.

Captain K. BRIDSON (50)

Born in 1935 at Douglas where he completed his education at the High School. In 1952 he commenced his sea-going career by going to the *Vindicatrix* Sea Training School. His first ship was the *Empress of Canada* and he was bridge boy when she caught fire in the Gladstone Dock. He then moved to Cunard's *Britannic* before joining Fyffes' banana boats. It was then to the Guinea Gulf Company for four years, on the *Robert L Holt* and *Elizabeth Holt* from where he obtained his 2nd Mate's and 1st Mate's Certificates. He joined the Steam Packet in 1961 as 2nd Officer, being promoted to Chief Officer in 1964.

> **Master: 1972   First Command: *Ramsey,* 1972**

His first passenger command came in 1974 with the *King Orry* (4) after which he was Master on all the Company ships in his time, on whatever rung of the ladder was required until 1985. After a heart attack he was advised to retire in 1986.

Ken Bridson is an extremely able, competent seaman and ship Master with a first-class mind. He obtained a BA degree from the Open University and happily is still to the fore.

Captain P. J. BRIDSON (19)

He was born in Castletown in 1893 and the first record of him in Steam Packet service was as an AB in 1913. He joined the Royal Navy in the First War and was at the Battle of Jutland. It was his claim to fame that he was the finest-looking matelot in the whole RN! He rejoined the Steam Packet in 1919 and was promoted to 2nd Mate a year later. He became Chief Officer in 1927. His officer service lasted until 1934.

> **Master: 1934 to 1958   First Command: *Peveril* (2)   Commodore: 1956 to 1958**

In 1939 he was commanding the *Victoria* which was then ninth in seniority of 16 ships. During the evacuations of May-June 1940 he was in the *Viking* which although bomb-damaged took part at the western ports of Le Havre, Cherbourg and famously, the evacuation of 1,800 children from St. Peter Port in Guernsey to Weymouth. He chose to leave in daylight as the *Viking's* funnels tended to 'fire up' at night and he considered it his responsibility to put the children first. In 2003 this action was commemorated in Guernsey.

After the war he took command of the new *Mona's Queen* in 1946, where the writer shared the honour, and the *Manxman* in 1955. As Commodore he took his flag to the *Ben-my-Chree* as she was always the favourite of that generation and considered as a 'kinder' ship.

Philip James Bridson was a fine seaman and an experienced ship Master. Familiarly known as 'Ginger' he was probably the greatest character ever to grace the bridge of a Steam Packet ship. He was an outward-going, avuncular man who always lived life to the full. In his earlier days he had been a keen sportsman and was one of the best centre forwards the Island has ever known. He carried that personality throughout his life and was known world-wide. In retirement he was always an attraction for his salty yarns when he served behind the bar at his daughter's hotel. He unfortunately did not enjoy a long retirement, passing away in 1964 aged 71.

Captain T.E. CAIN, DSC (28)

Born in Port St. Mary in 1886, Thomas Edwin Cain went to sea on the local fishing vessels and then on the schooners of which his father, 'Red Top' Cain, was owner/ skipper. He later obtained his certificates, joined the RNVR and during the First World War was commissioned as a Lieutenant in the Royal Navy where he was given the command of a Decoy Ship (Q ship).

In 1917 he had the distinction of destroying two enemy U boats for which he was awarded the DSC. For many other deeds, he was Mentioned in Dispatches no fewer than five times. After the war he resumed as Mate of the schooner *Venus* out of Port St. Mary, eventually becoming owner/ skipper himself. Then with the decline of this trade during the depression years, he joined the Steam Packet as 2nd Officer being promoted to Chief Officer in 1934. During the immediate pre-war period he served in the *King Orry* (3) but was in command of the *Ben-my-Chree* (4) during the Dunkirk evacuation where again he acquitted himself with honour before taking the damaged ship to Birkenhead. He then resumed as Chief Officer for the rest of the war joining the *Mona's Isle* (4) in 1945 with Captain Albert Whiteway when the writer (a kinsman) first set foot to work on an IOM boat. When the building of the new *King Orry* was completed in April 1946, he was her first Chief Officer and remained with her until ill health brought about his premature retirement.

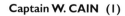

the captains

175

He was a brave man - there could not have been many Manxmen who were so highly commended in the wars. He could be a most compassionate man but he also possessed a fiery streak as anyone who crossed his bows could testify. He was also superstitious to such an extent that when travelling over the Fairy Bridge everyone, no matter who, in the railway carriage or on the bus had to doff their caps. He had a brother Leslie who was swept overboard and lost from the *Ben-my-Chree* (4) in 1929, a tragedy which affected him greatly.

His son John served with Hogarth's of Glasgow and achieved command with them. Tommy Cain went ashore in 1948 and died aged 64 in 1950.

Captain W. CAIN (1)

He was born in Douglas in about 1862. The first mention we have of him, care of Cecil Mitchell's notes, was that he joined the Company as a seaman in 1883, which puts him as born c1863. He obtained his certificates and was on the ladder as 2nd Mate and Mate until 1905 when he was promoted to Master.

Master: 1905 to 1932   First Command: *Ellan Vannin*

He was then in command on various of the junior passenger vessels pre-First War during which, in February 1917, he was Master of the paddle steamer *Mona's Queen* (2) when she was involved in an incident with the German Submarine UC.26. The U boat surfaced immediately ahead and the 'Queen's' port paddle box smashed her conning tower, damaging and disabling both her and unfortunately herself in the process. She was able to limp to Le Havre to land her troops and then made it back to Southampton for repairs. The event has gone down in Steam Packet annals and history as an illustrious event of the First War.

After the war and returning to normality, being now the Senior Master Capt. Cain was given command of the flagship *King Orry* (3) and was duly appointed Commodore. The following year he took over the newly acquired *Manxman* (1) and carried his flag on her until 1926. When the *Ben-my-Chree* (4) was built in 1927 he went there, still as Commodore and carried the burgee - the first of many on the ship. He continued as the 'Ben's' Master until August 1932 when he died suddenly while still in her command and the Company Commodore. Like his contemporaries he worked on to his 70's.

By what mentions there were of him in my time, William Cain was a fine seaman and ship's Master. He did not stop for much, weather and the likes did not bother him. His photo indicates a stern, fine-looking man every inch the part of a Commodore.

Captain L. CALLOW (32)

Born in 1905 at Douglas, most of his upbringing was on his Faragher grandparents' farm in Port St Mary. His Port St Mary background saw him go to sea as a boy on the local schooners *Venus* and *Progress* and then on coasters followed by six years as a seasonal seaman with the Steam Packet. He obtained his ticket and was appointed 2nd Mate in 1928. However, such was the way of life in those years of depression that he had to look elsewhere each winter. His officer service lasted from 1928 until 1945.

Master: 1946 to 1970   First Command: *Conister* (1), 1946
First passenger Command: *Victoria*, 1955   Commodore: 1969 - 1970

In 1939 he was Chief Officer of the *Victoria* but during the retreat from France he became Chief Officer of the *Manxman* (1), evacuating Dunkirk, Cherbourg and then St Malo where his Captain, P. B. Cowley was Mentioned in Dispatches. He then moved to various vessels on active duties throughout the war.

In 1946 he was promoted to Captain during the first peacetime season, and was Master of the *Conister* (1) for six years, then on each vessel according to his seniority of the era. His final five years were as Master of the *Lady of Mann* (1) and he was her last Commodore, taking his burgee there in season 1969. The writer was his Chief Officer. Professionally he was an excellent ship Master and a good teacher to his subordinates, never lacking in passing on his great experience. Of strong principles, he carried much authority and discipline. Lyndhurst Callow was a tall, dignified, fine-looking man with much personal presence and persona. He was a good-living, church-going person - a fine example and a good shipmate.

Among his many quotations is one that he attributed to Captain Bill Watson and which refers to the many Boards of Directors during his long service: "The Company is financially sound but socially bankrupt." Another which was often repeated was, "Penny wise but pound foolish!" These would be in reference to the low pay of those times! He used to remark that he could write a book about it all - and he could. A gregarious man, he loved to be surrounded by his friends of which he had many, regaling them with his salty yarns, both when on duty and in retirement.

He survived, wearing well to a grand age, dying aged 88 in 1993. To his friends he was 'Lyndie' but to we juniors he was still 'Sir' to the end, such was the respect he commanded.

Captain A. CLUCAS (39)

Alex Clucas was born in Douglas in 1905, the son of Capt. R. Clucas (Commodore from 1936/37) who was known as "The Shriker" and brother of Captain Bob Clucas. He first went to sea with Blue Funnel and joined the Steam Packet as a seaman in 1932, obtaining his ticket and being promoted to 2nd Mate of the *Mona* (4) in 1935. In the watershed year of 1939, he was 2nd Mate of the *Fenella* (2). He went to war with that vessel, experienced Dunkirk during which he was sent home to his father's funeral and missed the sinking. He was seconded out of the Company for most of the rest of the war serving with Coast Lines of Liverpool but returned to the Company in 1945 as 2nd Mate of the *Mona's Isle* (4). After this he became 2nd Mate of the new *King Orry* in April 1946 but was later promoted to Chief Officer of the *Peveril* in 1948. He then became the first Chief Officer on the new cargo ship *Fenella* (2) in 1952, then on each vessel in his turn during the 1950s.

> **Master: 1958 to 1961   First Command: *Conister* (1)**

Captain Clucas served as Master on cargo vessels until his untimely death on board the *Peveril* on 9th October 1961 at the age of 56. Alex Clucas was a Steam Packet man through and through, both from his family background and his own honourable service. His potential as a Master was never fully achieved. The writer served with him on the *Conister* where he was a fine seaman and ship handler and an excellent example to others, always encouraging junior colleagues to further their careers.

Captain R. CLUCAS (Snr) (4)

Capt. Clucas was from Douglas. The first record shows him as an AB in 1895. He was promoted to 2nd Mate in 1898 and to Chief Officer in 1906. In 1912 he was Chief Officer of the *Prince of Wales*.

> **Master: 1914   First Command: *Fenella* (1)   Fleet Commodore: 1936 to 1937, *Lady of Mann***

During the 1920s he was with the *Peel Castle* for several years and also the *King Orry* (3). In 1930 he was in the *Viking* and from 1933 until 1936 in the *Lady of Mann* (1).

He retired in April 1937 and died in May 1940. Like all his colleagues, not much was known about him in the writer's generation and he is better known as the father of Captain Bob (Junior) and Alex Clucas. It is also known that he died at the time of the Dunkirk evacuation and Admiral Ramsey would only allow one son home for the funeral. It therefore fell to Bob (Junior) to remain with the *Mona's Queen* in which he experienced and survived her sinking. Alex came home and missed the sinking of the *Fenella* in which he was the appointed 2nd Mate – his place being taken by Westby Kissack. Captain Robert (Senior) was also known as 'Bob' and was known as a fine ship handler and seaman. He was also known as 'The Shriker.'

Captain R. CLUCAS (Jnr) (31)

From Douglas where he was born in 1901, he hailed from the most traditional of Steam Packet families His father was Capt. Robert Clucas, known as "The Shriker" who was Fleet Commodore in 1936-37. Robert Jnr served foreign going as a seaman with Alfred Holts - Blue Funnel - and other companies. He worked for the Steam Packet as a seaman during the summer seasons, acquired his ticket and was appointed as 2nd Mate with the Steam Packet in the *Peel Castle* in 1927. His officer service lasted from 1927 until 1946.

> **Master: 1946 to 1964   First Command: *Peveril* (2)**
> **First passenger Command: *Manx Maid* (1), 1948**

In 1939 he was the Chief Officer of the *Mona's Queen* (3) going to war with that vessel on 3rd September, and when she was sunk on 29th May 1940 at Dunkirk he can be seen most prominently

175

in the ship's lifeboat of survivors in the Imperial War Museum photo of that incident. He continued as Chief Officer on various ships of the fleet for the duration of the war, mostly on the *Lady of Mann* (1) with Captain Tom Woods OBE. On the cessation of hostilities he was promoted Master in 1946. Thereafter he was Master on most of the Company's vessels according to his seniority of that generation and era. He brought the cargo vessel *Fenella* (3) from Troon in 1952. His last appointed command was the *Ben-my-Chree* (4) during the seasons 1962/ 63 by which time he was third in order of seniority of the fleet. He was a competent seaman and ship Master of great experience. His brother Alex was also a Steam Packet officer and Master. Bob Clucas was a friendly, outward-going, avuncular man of a portly stature and most popular with passengers. He always had a twinkle in the eye but could be a stern disciplinarian. He retired in 1964 and died in 1967, aged 66.

Captain C. H. COLLISTER (47)

He was born in Port St. Mary in 1928 and was another Steam Packet officer with previous family attachments. He went to sea as a boy with the IOM Harbour Board's ss *Mannin* before moving to the Ramsey Steamship Co and then joining the Steam Packet as an AB in 1952. On acquiring his Mate's ticket he moved to Coast Lines of Liverpool but joined the Company again as 2nd Mate in 1958.

> **Master: 1968 to 1977   First Command:** *Ramsey* **Assistant Marine Superintendent: 1973**
> **Marine Superintendent: 1977 to 1987**

Until going ashore, Capt. Collister served on every rung of the seniority ladder. Charles Harvey Collister was a hard-working officer and an excellent ship Master and handler. His final command was the *Mona's Queen* (5) and although there was no new tonnage during his period as Marine Superintendent, several second-hand ships came into the fleet under his aegis. These included the *Peveril* (4), the Company's first ro-ro vessel, the *Mona's Isle* (6) in 1985 and the *Tynwald* (6) in the same year.

With the startling decline in tourism during the 1980s, the Company underwent some drastic changes making his role even more onerous and stressful than before. He died suddenly, at Liverpool airport on 7th July 1987, aged 58 while on Company business and carrying out his duty.

Captain H. E. COLLISTER (43)

From Port St Mary, he was born at Cregneish in 1910, a member of a large and traditional seafaring family. He went to sea at a young age in coasters with firms such as the Zillah Steamship Company (Savages) of Liverpool. He joined the Steam Packet in 1936 as 2nd Mate of the *Mona* and in 1939 he was 2nd Mate of the *Victoria*. After the French evacuations and the loss of so many ships, along with most of the 2nd Mates he was seconded to other companies for the duration of the war. Among those companies were Stewarts of Glasgow and he was Mate there on *Yewmount*, also seeing service in tankers. He returned to the Steam Packet in 1946 as 2nd Mate of the *Manx Maid* (1) and was thereafter on every rung of the ladder as 2nd Mate. He was the first 2nd Mate on the new cargo vessel *Fenella* (3) in 1952 then 2nd Mate of the *Lady of Mann* (1) in 1955 with the writer as AB. He was promoted to Chief Officer of the *Peveril* (2) in 1957. He was for two years the senior Company Chief Officer on the *Lady of Mann* during 1963 to1964.

> **Master: 1965   First Command:** *Ramsey*

He had a short career in command going ashore in the same year. Harry Collister was a fine seaman and officer of great experience. He was holder of both a Master's Certificate and the Liverpool Licence and later worked with the Liverpool University Marine Biological Station at Port Erin. He retired to his home in Port St Mary.

Captain J. F. COLLISTER (22)

Another from the Port St Mary school of navigators, Captain Collister was born in 1883 and was from an established family of seafarers. His elder brother William was also a Steam Packet Master. After a traditional early career in fishing boats and coasters he joined the Steam Packet as 2nd Mate in 1913. The First War interfered with his career, as it did with so many of his generation, and he was seconded to other companies where he became a Master. He rejoined the Fleet in 1919. Promoted to Chief Officer: 1928. Officer service 1913/1919 to 1935.

> **Master: 1936 to 1948   First Command:** *Conister* (1)

During 1937 he was in command of the *Peel Castle*, in 1938 the *Rushen Castle*, and in 1939 - the watershed year - in command of the *Manx Maid* (1). He was in various commands during the Second World War resuming his first peacetime year in 1946 on the *Mona's Isle* (4).

He completed the last two years of his career on the first *Manxman*, which was still under Ministry of War Transport control and running between Harwich and the Hook of Holland.

James Frederick Collister was a fine seaman of great experience and an excellent ship handler from the old school of merchantmen. Everyone knew him simply as Fred.

Captain J. J. COMISH (5)

From Kirk Michael, where he was born in 1867. The first Company record of him dates from 1890 when he was an AB. He was later promoted to 3rd Mate of the *Mona's Queen* (2) in 1906 and 2nd Mate two years later. By 1911 he was Chief Officer of the *Queen Victoria* and then in 1913 transferred to the new *King Orry* (3) with his uncle, Capt. J.J. Bridson as Master. He served on the *Mona's Queen* during the First War, returning to the *King Orry* in 1919.

> Promoted Master: 1920   First Command: *Mona's Queen* (2)   Fleet Commodore: 1937 to 1938

In the 1920s he was on the *Peel Castle* and *Rushen Castle* but moved to the *King Orry* in 1930 followed by the *Manxman*. In 1934, when in his 67th year, he brought out the new *Mona's Queen* (3) but in 1936 moved to the *Ben-my-Chree* (4) and was appointed Commodore in April 1937. The photograph had to be taken at that time.

John Comish (or Comaish as he was known to the older Manx sailormen) was a fine looking but austere man, very much revered and looking the part of a 1930s ship Master. The writer's father served with him on the new *Mona's Queen* in 1935 and his voice would drop octaves when speaking of Captain Comaish.

He retired at the end of the 1938 season aged 71 and died in 1940.

Captain T. L. CORKILL (26)

He was born in 1903 at Laxey. After a hard upbringing he worked in the Laxey mines and then went to sea with the Ramsey Steamship Co, the Steam Packet and Blue Funnel from where obtained his 2nd Mate's Certificate. He joined the Steam Packet as 2nd Mate in 1928 and was promoted Chief Officer in 1933. His Officer service lasted from 1928 to 1938/46 – a period of 18 years.

Master: 1938. First Command: *Conister* (1) for one year only. On the sale of *Peel Castle* and the *Mona* he had to revert to Mate.

> Master (Full): 1946 to 1956   First Command: *Manx Maid* (1)
> Appointed Assistant Marine Superintendent: 1947   Marine Superintendent: 1957 to 1968

In 1939 he was Chief Officer of the *Ben-my-Chree* (4) and remained with her throughout the war. He was promoted to Master in 1946. Thereafter he served as Master according to his rank and as Assistant Marine Superintendent, his last seagoing command being the *Ben-my-Chree* (which was the second ship of the fleet at that time) in 1955 and 1956.

Thomas Leslie Corkill was a good-living competent man, cool in temperament, an excellent ship Master and handler. As such he graced whatever bridge he commanded.

As Marine Superintendent he oversaw the building of the *Manx Maid* (2) in 1962 which was probably the most innovative ship ever to serve and which saved both the Company and Manx tourism at that time. She was followed by the *Ben-my-Chree* (5) in 1966 - a fine sister ship, both from Cammell Laird. The cargo motor vessels *Peveril* (3) in 1964 and *Ramsey* in 1965 were built at the Ailsa yard at Troon.

T. L. Corkill was a respected boss, known either as 'TL' or Tom but to we junior ranks always as 'The Super' or indeed as 'Sir'. It was he who gave our generation the chance of a career with the home company. He retired in 1968 and died in 1983 aged 80.

Captain B. C. CORLETT (41)

His father was a schoolmaster and he was born at Port St. Mary in 1906. He went to sea as a cadet in 1922 and joined the Steam Packet as 2nd Mate in 1936 before moving to a position with the IOM Harbour Board and rejoining in fleet in 1938. In 1939 he was Mate in the *Cushag* and then served at the evacuations of the French ports as 3rd Mate in the *Lady of Mann* (1). Like all other junior officers, he was seconded out for the duration of the war but he returned as 3rd Mate of the *Ben-my-Chree* (4) in 1946. The following year he was 2nd Mate on the *Viking* before being promoted to Chief Officer in 1953.

Officer service: 1936 to 1961   Master: 1961 to 1971   First Command: *Conister* (1)

He was in the cargo section for six years and was first Master of the *Ramsey* in 1965. His first passenger command was the *King Orry* (4) in 1967 after which he served on all the ships in the fleet ending with the *Mona's Isle* (5) in 1971 from which he retired.

Basil Christian Corlett was a tall, placid, good-living and retiring man and was always a joy to sail with. He was full of anecdotes and was most resourceful – it was said of him that he could have even scratched a living on Kitterland*. He was made Senior Master rather late in his career but he coped magnificently. In retirement he loved his country walks and always had a dog. His Christian name was Basil by which he was always known. He was another founder of the Mariners' Choir and died in 1988 at the age of 82. (* *the small island in Calf Sound*)

Captain P. C. CORRIN (57)

He was born in 1949 at Port St Mary into a family with a strong nautical background. His father was Master on the Ramsey Steamship vessels and from there he acquired his seagoing nurture. After education at Castle Rushen High School he did a summer season as a junior rating with the Steam Packet but went to sea with the Ramsey Steamship Company as a seaman learning his trade and nautical skills around the Irish Sea waters. He joined the Steam Packet in 1969 as a seaman on *The Ramsey* acquiring his tickets and being promoted to 2nd Mate in 1971. He stood on all rungs of the ladder as 2nd Mate and Chief Officer. His officer service lasted 8 years.

Master: 1978   First Command: *Conister* (2)   First passenger Command: *Mona's Isle* (5), 1980
Marine Superintendent   Marine Operations Manager

Thereafter from 1978, he served on whatever ship he was required to work in and was the last Master of the *Manxman* (2) in 1982. He was appointed Marine Superintendent in 1987 and has overseen the introduction into the fleet of fast craft and the building and introduction of the *Ben-my-Chree* (6) in 1998.

Peter Carine Corrin is a fine seaman and an excellent ship Master and handler. He is a most worthy successor to his predecessors in a most difficult era and a credit to his cloth, being a fine example of the best traditions of the Steam Packet and Manx seafaring. In such hands the continuation of the Company is assured.

Captain T. H. CORTEEN (38)

From Douglas where he was born in 1907, he later went to sea as a boy on the schooner *Venus* with Capt. T. Cain, DSC and with local coasters before sailing deep water with Blue Funnel. There he obtained Foreign Going Certificates before joining the Steam Packet in 1932 as a seaman during the depression years. He was promoted to 2nd Mate on the *Rushen Castle* in 1934 and was promoted to Chief Officer in 1947. Officer service: 1934 to 1948 - 14 years.

Master: 1960 to 1972   First Command: *Conister* (1)
First passenger Command: *King Orry*, 1962

In 1939 he was 2nd Mate on the *Manxman* (1), serving at Dunkirk and other areas of the evacuation. After the loss of so many ships in 1940 he was seconded from the Steam Packet along with almost all the 2nd Mates for the duration of the war and saw active service in the Far East theatre of war. He rejoined the fleet in 1946 as 2nd Mate of the *Ben-my-Chree* (4). From 1948 he was promoted to Chief Officer for 12 years and was later also 12 years in command. During his years in command he was Master on all ships of the fleet, the last two seasons being in command of the flagship *Lady of*

Mann (1) as Senior Sailing Master. Indeed he was the last Master on arguably that finest of all the ships (era for era) built for the Steam Packet. Tommy Corteen was an excellent seaman and a ship Master of much experience. He possessed a fine brain but was not a big man (of James Cagney proportions and characterisations) but to those who knew him he was a man born before his time and a good shipmate. He had a by-name of "The Beau" carried from his younger days. He retired in January 1972 and remained a regular member of the Mariners' Choir. He died in 1995 aged 88.

Captain S. T. COWIN (58)

He was born at Douglas in 1949 and educated at Douglas High School. Later he went to sea as a cadet with Elder Dempster Lines of Liverpool. After acquiring his 2nd Mate's Certificate he sailed for a while with that company, joining the Steam Packet as 2nd Mate in 1970. Chief Officer 1976. Officer service 8 years.

> **Master: 1978   First Command: *Conister* (2)**

His first passenger command was the *Manxman* (2) in 1982 and thereafter he served where required. He is at present the Senior Sailing Master of the *Ben-my-Chree* (6) and is another fine example of a Manx seaman, officer and ship's Master within the best traditions of our calling.

175

Captain P. B. COWLEY (16)

Captain Phillip Basil Cowley was a native of Peel where he was born in 1891. He joined the Steam Packet in 1919 after service in the Royal Navy during the First World War. Later obtaining his Certificates, he was promoted to 2nd Mate in 1924 and to Chief Officer during 1927.

> **First Command: *Peveril* (2), 1933   First passenger Command: *Manx Maid* (1), 1934**
> **Commodore: 1955 to 1957**

Captain Cowley was in command of the *Manxman* (1) at the evacuation of Dunkirk which was followed by the north-western French ports of Cherbourg and St Malo, where he earned his citation. Rommel referred to the *Manxman*, then under the command of Captain Cowley, as "that cheeky two-funnelled steamer," so close was she to the advancing German army.

After the war Captain Cowley was in command of the *Lady of Mann* (1), the Company's senior vessel, from 1946 to 1957 and was Fleet Commodore in the period from 1955 until January 1957. He was an autocratic man (the last of his type) but a fine ship handler and a competent ship Master. He was always known as 'PB' although in his younger days he enjoyed the sobriquet of 'Peter the Painter', being apprenticed to that trade before going to sea. He did not live long in retirement: like so many of his generation he was a heavy smoker and it was said that he could polish off a packet of 20 'Gold Flake' between the Lune Buoy and the berth at Fleetwood. He died in December 1960.

Captain J. D. CRAINE (36)

From Colby where he was born in 1903. His father was Station Master at Colby which was an eminent position at that time. After working on farms he went to sea at a young age on the schooner *Venus*, out of Port St Mary. As a seaman, he served in local coasters and also foreign-going with Booths of Liverpool. Service with the Steam Packet began as a seaman in the late 1920s and he was promoted to 2nd Mate of the *Mona's Isle* (4) in 1933.

> **Master: 1957 to 1968   First Command: *Conister* (1)   First passenger Command: *King Orry* (4), 1960**

In 1939 he was 2nd Mate on the *Ben-my-Chree* (4) but being RNR was called to the 'colours' from 1940 to 1945 seeing much active service. His last RN duty was as Camp Chief Petty Officer at Ronaldsway but in 1946 he resumed his Steam Packet career on 'demob' as Chief Officer of the *Manx Maid* (1). Thereafter he stepped on all rungs of the ladder as Mate and was Senior Company Chief Officer during 1955/ 56. He was Master in cargo ships from 1957 to 1959 and on passenger vessels from 1960 to 1968, his last command being the *Manxman* (2) of which he was extremely proud, she being in his eye still a new ship. He called his house the same. He was a much-respected gentleman by his subordinates and a good shipmate. Johnny Craine was a fine sailor and ship Master. He lived in Castletown for his entire Steam Packet career but sadly his health soon failed and he died in 1974, aged 71.

Captain T. K. CRELLIN (55)

From Douglas where he was born in 1944. He went to sea as an apprentice cadet with Elder Dempster Lines of Liverpool from 1962 to 1966 and joined the Steam Packet in 1966 as 2nd Mate. He served as Chief Officer from 1969 to 1976.

First Command: *Conister* (2), **1977**

He joined Manx Line and was Master of the *Manx Viking* from 1978 until 1985. After the merger in 1985, Ken Crellin resumed his career with the Steam Packet and commanded the Senior vessels of his day: *Tynwald* (6), *King Orry* (5) and *Ben-my-Chree* (6).

A most efficient marine officer and a gentleman, he gives whatever duty he has to do a hundred per cent. He retired in 2002 but still does the occasional summer relief on the *Ben-my-Chree*. At the time of his retirement he was the Senior Sailing Master.

Captain W. H. CRELLIN (24)

A native of Peel, he was born in 1900 and was a product of the local herring fleet. After the First War he joined the Steam Packet as an AB and was promoted to 2nd Mate in 1925. His officer service covered the period from 1925 to 1936.

First Command: *Peveril* (2), **1937** then *Rushen Castle* the same year   **Master: 1937 to 1960**

In 1939 he was Master of the *Peveril* but then took various commands and positions for the duration of the war, mostly on cargo vessels. In 1946 he moved to the *Mona's Isle* (4) during which time the writer served with him. Captain Crellin was the recognised Master of the *Viking* for some years and is still remembered at Fleetwood.

William Herbert Crellin (known as 'Herbie') was a most competent and experienced seaman of a unique character and strong religious belief. It was an enquiry from a long-ago passenger who sent a copy of his photograph to Imperial Buildings for identification that initiated this whole exercise.

Herbie died in 1960 aged 60 while still in harness as Master of the *Ben-my-Chree* (4). At the time of his death he was the fleet's Second Senior Master and had held command for 23 years.

Captain J. W. CUBBON (15)

He was born in Douglas in 1890 and his early seagoing career was as a seaman in the foreign and coasting trades, including the Steam Packet. He joined the Steam Packet as 2nd Mate in 1920 and his officer service lasted from 1920 until 1932. He was the first Chief Officer on the new *Ben-my-Chree* (4) in 1927.

Master: 1933 to 1954   First Command: 1933 *Conister* (1) and *Peel Castle* - the same year
Commodore: 1946 to 1955

In 1939 he was Master of the *Manxman* (1)which was the then sixth senior vessel of the fleet as was his ranking. He was in command of the *Fenella* (2) when she was sunk at Dunkirk and was rescued off the beaches after being blown up again on the *Crested Eagle*. He then served on various commands throughout the war where and when required. Up to his time, he was the longest-serving Commodore in the Fleet's history and chose the *Ben-my-Chree* (4) as his Flagship, which was the junior ship to the *Lady of Mann* (1). By all accounts the 'Ben' was a "kinder" ship. A quiet, unassuming and modest man for his position, he was known as Walter but more affectionately to the crews as 'Wangle'. He went ashore in January 1955 and enjoyed a good retirement.

Captain R. M. DICKINSON (52)

Born at Ulverston in 1933, his parents came to the IOM in the licensed trade, first to Sulby Glen and then to the Peveril Hotel at Peel. His formative and school years were in Peel and at the High School, Douglas. He then went to HMS *Conway* Sea Training School in 1947 and after passing out served his cadetship with Clan Line. He was an officer with Canadian Pacific and then Lamport & Holt of Liverpool. On obtaining his Master's Certificate, he joined the Steam Packet as 2nd Mate on the *Manxman* (2) in1963 being promoted to Chief Officer in 1966.

First Command: *Conister* (2), **1974   First passenger Command:** *Snaefell* (5), **1976**

In 1978 Captain Dickinson joined Manx Line and was in command of the *Manx Viking* until 1985 when the companies merged. He returned to the Steam Packet colours on the *Tynwald* (6) and other vessels as required. Although a fine figure of a man, Ray Dickinson retired on medical advice in 1978.

He still lived in Peel where he was on the lifeboat committee and enjoyed his walks along the prom looking out towards the western sea, often chatting with his old shipmates. He died in February 2000, aged 67.

Captain C. DUGGAN (62)

From Douglas where he was born in 1949 into the most traditional of Steam Packet families - his grandfather being Captain Radcliffe Duggan DSC. After a Manx education he joined the Royal Navy as a boy rating in 1964 remaining there for ten years. He joined the Steam Packet in 1974 as an AB but got his ticket and was promoted to 2nd Mate in 1975 becoming Chief Officer of the *Mona's Isle* (5) in 1977. His officer service was between 1975 and 1988 - 13 years.

> Master: 1988   First Command: *Peveril* (4)

Thereafter he served as Master on whichever vessel was rostered: *Peveril* (4), *King Orry* (5), *Belard* and *Lady of Mann* (2) along with the *SeaCat Isle of Man* and *SeaCat Danmark*. He was with SeaCats from the first year of their introduction into Steam Packet service. These days he takes his turn on the *Ben-my-Chree* (6) and the other units of the fleet as required.

Colin Duggan is another who has come up through the well-tried and traditional route and has brought to the Steam Packet his long seafaring expertise: the best type of Manx seaman, officer and Master

Captain R. DUGGAN, DSC (14)

From Port St Mary where he was born in 1880, he went to sea as a boy in the 19th century herring fleet and was ship's cook in the 'Nickies', such was the pattern of life in those days. The writer's grandfather was skipper on his first boat. His service with the Steam Packet started as a seaman before the First War; the records show him working for the Company as from 1907. His officer career with the Company lasted from 1920 until 1929.

> Master: 1929 to 1945   First Command: *Tyrconnel*

He was engaged on all rungs of the passenger ship ladder in the '30s from the *Mona* (4) to the *King Orry* (3). He came to the *Mona's Queen* (3), then the third senior vessel, in 1938. In 1939 he became Master of the *Mona's Queen* (3) and went to war with her in September 1939 first serving as a troop carrier out of Southampton and operating in the Western Channel and North Sea. He then took the ship with the first flotilla into Dunkirk under strong enemy attack and took out as many troops as she could carry. He was then relieved and went ashore but on the ship's return to Dunkirk under Captain A. Holkham, she was sunk. Thereafter during the remainder of the war Captain Duggan was Master of the *Ben-my-Chree* (4) mostly in northern waters which included running as far as Iceland and regularly to the Faeroes. Also, along with the *Lady of Mann* (1), she was engaged offloading American troops from the liners, including the Cunard Queens, at the Tail of the Bank and in Belfast Lough. He took a prominent part in the D. Day landings, notably the landings at Omaha Beach with the US Army Rangers. He was later decorated with the Distinguished Service Cross for his gallantry and leadership. Records also inform us he was Mentioned in Dispatches no fewer than six times and became a personal friend of Field Marshal Montgomery. His grandson Colin is a present Master with the Company which illustrates that we are still very much a family concern.

Radcliffe Duggan was a fine seaman of the "old school." An autocratic man, as they all were and entitled to be, he was better known by all who knew of him as 'The Rajah'. He died in 1957 aged 77.

Captain E. C. FARGHER (49)

Born into an established Steam Packet family at Douglas in 1936. He went to sea straight from school with Alfred Holt's Blue Funnel Line from where he obtained his Foreign Going Certificates and joined the Steam Packet 1961 as 2nd Mate on the *Tynwald* (5). He was later the first 2nd Mate on the new *Manx Maid* in 1962 and was promoted to Chief Officer in 1963.

> Master: 1971 to 1998   First Command: *Ramsey*   Commodore: 1989 to 1998

He was Master on all rungs of the ladder in his generation – the *Ramsey* to *King Orry* (4) to the *Ben-my-Chree* (6), completing 27 years in command. Edward Fargher was a fine seaman and ship handler, much respected by his crews and the travelling public. In the early days of the relieving system he accepted the challenge of going round the vessels of the fleet in the height of the busy summer schedule, thus allowing us all a much-appreciated break. Of all the innovations of modern times the summer relief system had to be favourite. An outward-going persona and handsome with it, if any one of us could claim the title of debonair, ECF it would have to be!

He retired as Commodore in 1998.

Captain E. Q. FARRINGTON (25)

Born in Laxey c1889, he was foreign-going in his youth and acquired Foreign Going Certificates. Captain Farrington belonged to an established Manx family. His uncle J.R. Quayle was Deputy Chairman of the Steam Packet from the 1940s until the 1960s while at the same time holding the post of Chairman of the IOM Bank which probably made him the most powerful man in the IOM at that time! Edward Farrington joined the Steam Packet in 1928 as 2nd Mate and was promoted to Chief Officer in 1933.

Master: 1937 to 1940   First Command: *Conister* (1)

During the war, with the loss of so many ships, he had to revert to Chief Officer and at the cessation of hostilities he decided to remain as such, declining further command. He finished his career with the Steam Packet as Chief Officer on the *Manxman* (1) then still on active post-war service with the Ministry of War Transport. Retiring in 1948, Edward Quayle Farrington was a quiet, unassuming man usually known as 'Ted' but more popularly as 'Yah-Yah', apparently because of the manner of his speech. He died in 1962, aged 73.

Captain W. GAWNE (2)

From Peel, he was born c1870. The first record of his Steam Packet service was in 1896 as an AB on the *Ben-my-Chree* (2). In 1901 he was 2nd Mate on the ps *Mona's Queen* and 1908 on the new *Ben-my-Chree* (3) where he must have been her first 2nd Mate. By 1909 he was Chief Officer on the ps *Empress Queen.*

Master: 1912 to 1932   First Command: *Douglas* (3)

During the First War he was noted as in command of the *Douglas* (3) and *Fenella* (1). Then in 1919 he was on the *Peel Castle* still trooping from Southampton. By 1926 he was serving on board the *Viking* which was then No 2 ship and held second position in seniority. Captain Gawne's big moment must have been during 1930 when he was given command of the new *Lady of Mann* (1). He kept in her charge through to 1932 when he is recorded as retiring at the end of the year. He died on 30th September 1936 and is buried at Douglas.

Not a great deal has been passed on concerning his character but he was obviously a man of great seafaring and Steam Packet experience and extremely well-respected in his time.

Captain R. E. GELLING (34)

From Laxey but born at Santon in 1897. He joined the Steam Packet in 1911 as a boy rating. After service as a seaman with the Company, he served in the Royal Navy during World War 1 and later became a policeman at Barrow. Returning to the Steam Packet in the 1920s, he obtained his certificates and became 2nd Mate in 1927, being appointed to the new *Peveril* (2) in 1929. His officer service spanned 26 years.

Master: 1953 to 1962.   First Command: *Conister* (1)   First passenger Command: *King Orry* (4), 1957

In 1939 he was Chief Officer of the *Viking* which rescued 1,800 children from St Peter Port, Guernsey. One story of his concerned a lady escort for these children who forgot to lock the door of her house, gave him the keys and asked him to lock up when they went back! Shortly after that the Germans landed on Guernsey and those keys, I understand, are still in the Gelling family's possession. He later served on various ships of the fleet as and where required but mostly on the *Victoria*. He was the first Chief Officer of the new *Mona's Queen* in 1946 and then the *Snaefell* in 1948. He was then the Senior Chief Officer until 1953 when he was promoted to Master although he was not long Master by Steam Packet standards - 9 years - but during this time he acquitted himself with distinction.

Eddie Gelling, better known as 'Ned,' had a long Steam Packet career from 1911 to 1962. He was a

quiet, kindly, good-living man and a fine seaman of much experience. He was given to expressing himself in the old Manx Gaelic which included the occasional helm and bridge orders! The writer was his 2nd Mate on the *Tynwald* (5) during the 1960 season and also had been with him in the *Mona's Queen* (4) when new in 1946 and the *Peveril* (2) in 1955-57 - a kindly, proper gent to sail with who encouraged young seamen to study for their tickets. He had a deserved long and quiet retirement and died in 1982, aged 85.

Captain F. GRIFFIN (35)

Born in 1908 at Port Erin, he came from farming stock going to sea as a boy in Manx coasters. He then went foreign going as a seaman and after passing his 2nd Mate's Foreign Going Certificate became an officer with Liverpool's Booth Line. He joined the Steam Packet as 2nd Mate in 1933.

> Master: 1955 to 1967
> First Command: *Conister* (1)   Appointed Assistant Marine Superintendent: 1965
> Marine Superintendent: 1968 to 1973

In 1939 he was 2nd Mate on the *Lady of Mann* (1) but as a RNR officer he was called up and given command of Fleet Auxiliary vessels in Home Waters and the Far East. After cessation of hostilities he rejoined the Company as Chief Officer of the *Rushen Castle*. He became Senior Company Chief Officer on the *Lady of Mann* in 1953/ 54. In 1964 he brought out the new cargo ship *Peveril* as Master.

As Marine Superintendent he oversaw the building of the *Mona's Queen* (5) at Troon. She was the Company's first motor-engined passenger vessel and was probably the finest handling purpose-built ship the Company ever had to that time.
Frank Griffin was a cool, competent man and an excellent ship Master and handler. He had much personal tragedy losing two children at a young age, a tragedy he met with much fortitude. He survived to have a fair retirement and was one of the founders of the Mariners' Choir with which he worked hard to make it the success it became. He died in 1989, aged 81.

Captain D. C. HALL (53)

A native of Whitley Bay, Northumberland, the second of our Masters to originate from that county, finding their way to the Isle of Man through family circumstances. David Hall served his cadetship with a north-east firm and joined the Steam Packet as 2nd Mate in 1963 on the *Snaefell* (5), when the writer was his Chief Officer. Promoted to Chief Officer 1967.

> Master: 1975 to 1985 First Command: *Conister* (2)

He was Master on passenger vessels from 1977 and thereafter in his time on all of the Company's ships, both passenger and cargo, until his retirement through ill health in 1985.
David Courtney Hall, an urbane gentleman and a fine sailor from an established north east family, was a competent ship's Master.
It was with great sadness that during the final editing of this chapter, he passed away, aged 71, in January 2005.

Captain T. E. HARRISON (69)

He was born at Fleetwood in 1939 where he grew up and was educated in the fishing town. From school he went to sea in the local trawler fleet with his ship-master uncles who taught him the rudiments of seamanship and navigation. This was then the accepted and traditional path to sea of the fishing peoples of the Lancashire port. When the Icelandic Cod War threatened their livelihoods, these men had to seek work elsewhere and it was at that time - 1964 – that Tom Harrison sought pastures new on the Isle of Man by taking a skipper's job on the newly built Warrior-class boats out of Port St Mary, fishing for scallops. Moving on from there, he then skippered the mfv *Essex Girl* tendering to 'Radio Caroline' in Ramsey Bay He then moved to Peel where he was given charge of the mv *Vingafjord* bringing in food cargoes from Portavogie in Northern Ireland. It was after this he joined the Steam Packet as a seaman and it was not long before he was made bosun. The writer had the benefit of his experience on the *Manxman* in 1975. Shortly after that time he decided to enrol at the Fleetwood School of Navigation and achieved success in obtaining his certificates. He was immediately promoted to 2nd Mate with the Company in 1977 and made up to Chief Officer in 1985. His officer service extended for over 20 years.

> First Command: *Lady of Mann* (2) and also had charge of the *Ben-my-Chree* (6).

175

Tom Harrison is a fine seaman and officer of much experience who acquitted himself as Master with distinction later in life than most, which gives all the more credit to him. This also applied to the many challenges of his long seagoing career and he blended better than most into the Steam Packet scene. He still does the occasional summer relief with the Company. A collector of Steam Packet memorabilia, his archive would grace the museum. Among his other interests is collecting for seafaring charities and in the shore-side world, raising funds for TT safety. In all he has raised hundreds of thousands of pounds for those and other charities, a commendable effort from a dedicated and talented person - worthy of greater recognition!

Captain A. HOLKHAM (17)

Captain Holkham was from Bognor Regis in Sussex where he was born in 1886. He came to the Isle of Man as 2nd Mate with the *Onward*, later the *Mona's Isle* (4), in 1920. He met a Manx girl and stayed, seeing service with the Steam Packet as an officer from 1920 to 1933 and becoming Chief Officer in 1928. He was the first Chief Officer of the new *Lady of Mann* in 1930.

> **Master: 1933 to 1945. First Command: *Conister* (I)**

Season 1939: Master of *King Orry* (3), the eighth in seniority of the 16 ships in the fleet. He was relief Master on the *Mona's Queen* (4) when she was blown up at Dunkirk before serving on various ships of the fleet during the war, mainly in the *Viking* but also on home service with the *Snaefell* (4) and *Rushen Castle*. By all accounts, from those who remember him, he was a fine upstanding man and an excellent ship handler, being both quiet and efficient by nature. He was probably the only non-Manx officer of that era who made it to Master. He acquitted himself well. Archibald Holkham was usually known as 'Archie'. After a hectic war service, he retired early in 1945 aged 59 and died aged 75 in 1961.

Captain J. J. KEIG (13)

From The Howe, Port St Mary where he was born in 1889. He went to sea as a boy with the fishing fleet as so many of his generation from the south of the Island. He then sailed out of Liverpool on coastwise vessels with the writer's father. He was with the Steam Packet as a seaman from before the First War and joined as an officer after the war, his service as 2nd Mate commencing from 1919. He was promoted to Chief Officer in 1924.

> **Master: 1928 First Command: *Fenella* (1)**

He was Master throughout the 1930s taking command of the new *Tynwald* (4) in 1937. He was in that ship during 1939 and was then the third senior Master of the fleet. During the time of Dunkirk he was in command of the *Victoria* when she was on the home run to Liverpool. He was with her when she was mined off the Mersey Bar in December 1940 after which she was able to make port and saw out the war. After this and other incidents, the home run moved to the somewhat safer port of Fleetwood. He was also in command of the *Victoria* at the D-Day landings in June 1944 landing British and US assault forces on the western edge of the Arromanches area. He held that command until the cessation of hostilities.

There is a commemorative tray that used to adorn the Master's room in the *Mona's Queen* (5) showing Captain Keig and his officers to the fore. Taking ill at the end of the war he sadly died in November 1945 from what is believed to have been the result of war-time stress: aged only 55.

In the 1950s and 60s he had two sons John and Tom in the fleet. John became a senior Chief Officer and was later Harbour Master at Douglas. Captain Jack Keig was a fine figure of a man, probably the tallest at any time to grace the bridge of a Steam Packet vessel. A first class mariner, ship handler and much respected, had he survived he would have been the Senior Master in the period 1946 - 1955.

Captain J. KELLY (68)

Born in 1951 in Liverpool and grew up in the Huyton district of the city where he was educated at St Dominic's and later, in 1967, the Gravesend Sea Training School in Kent. He first went to sea with Elder Dempster Lines for three years on the *Apapa* and *Accra*. Then as was the pattern with us all working with the various and established old Liverpool firms of Cunard, Alfred Holt (Blue Funnel) and Ellermans, he obtained his certificates and joined the Steam Packet as 2nd Mate in 1979 becoming Chief Officer during 1988. His officer service extended for 20 years.

> **Master: 1999 to date First Command: *SeaCat Isle of Man***

He is now one of the Masters of the *Ben-my-Chree* (6). Like most of his predecessors, John Kelly came along the traditional route from seaman and officer to Master, gathering much nautical experience along the way.

Captain J. S. KENNAUGH (45)

He was born in 1932 at Red Gap, Castletown and educated locally at King William's College. He went to sea as a cadet and officer with Lamport and Holt of Liverpool before joining the Steam Packet as 2nd Mate on the *Victoria* in 1956. His service as officer lasted from 1956 until 1966 before becoming first Chief Officer on the *Ben-my-Chree* (5) in 1966.

Master: 1967 to 1987   First Command: *Ramsey*   Commodore: 1973 to 1987

He served as officer and Master on all of the Company's ships in his time. In 1976 he brought the new *Lady of Mann* (2) from Troon, which had to be the highlight of an illustrious career. He also brought to the Company's service the *Antrim Princess* later to be renamed *Tynwald* (6) in 1985. Captain Kennaugh was a precise and fine seaman and an excellent ship Master and was the longest serving Commodore in the Company's history: 14 years to Captain JW Cubbon's 8 years. John Shore Kennaugh was known by his Christian name John but as with all exacting persons, he carried several sobriquets!

He retired prematurely in 1987 and died aged 59 in 1991.

Captain J. H. KERRUISH (29)

Captain Kerruish was with the Steam Packet as a seaman from the 1920s, obtaining his certificates and being promoted to 2nd Mate during the late 1920s. He was the first 2nd Mate of the new *Lady of Mann* in 1930.

Promoted to Chief Officer in 1936

He was never fully appointed as Master but took command of the *Manx Maid* (1) during the evacuation of France where he acquitted himself with distinction. He retired from the Company in 1946 and thereafter worked ashore with the Manx Electric Railway.

Captain C.A. KINLEY (7)

Born in 1890 at Surby, Port Erin from a Manx seafaring family, Crawford Kinley went to sea as a boy with his father (known as 'Neddy Dickie') in the Port St Mary herring fleet. He then served in coastwise ships out of Liverpool, namely Zillah Steamship Company's - Savages' ss *Sarah Brough* with the writer's father. His brother John was 2nd Mate of the ill-fated *Ellan Vannin* that was lost in 1909. He joined the Steam Packet as a seaman and was promoted to 2nd Mate in 1913. He was then seconded out of the Company for a while in the First War but rejoined the fleet in 1919 and was appointed to command in 1920.

Master: 1920 to 1933   First Command: *Cushag*   Marine Superintendent: 1933 to 1956

Appointed Marine Superintendent in December 1933, he was the first marine officer to hold the position full-time in the Company history. Thereafter Captain Kinley remained on shore in charge of all Marine Operations and before the Second War oversaw the building of three new ships. He continued in charge of the Company's ships and personnel during the years of hostilities. From 1945 he oversaw the rebuilding of the fleet with six new passenger vessels constructed at Cammell Laird, Birkenhead and one cargo ship, the *Fenella* (3), at Troon.

As Superintendent it could be said he kept a tight ship and was always his own man, small of stature but with a strong personality, Captain Kinley's Christian names were Crawford Albert but he was always referred to as 'Crawfie'. However, to the old Manx seamen of his generation he was still 'Neddy Dickie's' son and known by that. His brother Hugh was also the senior ship's Master with John Stewarts of Glasgow and was decorated for his wartime services. The writer served with him in that company. Captain Crawford Kinley retired in 1956 and was for a while a Douglas Town Councillor. He survived well into retirement and died aged 83 in December 1974.

Captain G. R. KINLEY (23)

Born in 1900 at Port St Mary, he came from a seafaring background as all young men from that little port did in those generations. He went to sea as a boy with the fishing fleet and then as a seaman with Wilson's of Whitehaven. He joined the Steam Packet as an officer in 1923 and was made Chief Officer in 1928.

Master: 1937 to 1965   First Command: *Conister* (1)   Commodore: 1958 to 1965

In 1939 he was Master on the *Rushen Castle*. During the war he served on whatever ship was required and spent some time on the home service with the *Snaefell* (4) and *Rushen Castle*. On cessation of hostilities in 1946, he resumed his rank of seniority as Master of the *Victoria* also serving in the *Manxman* (1) at Harwich. Thereafter he took his place on each rung of the ladder until 1957 when he became a Master of the fleet flagship *Lady of Mann* (1) becoming Commodore from 1958 to 1965 and carrying his flag on the 'Lady.'.

George Redvers Kinley was a fine upstanding man and an excellent seaman of great experience, holding his commands and Commodore's position with much dignity and was always an extremely conscientious and dedicated officer. He was one of two brothers who, with a nephew, all became Masters in the fleet.

A clean-living, church-going man all his seafaring life, in retirement he was Church Warden of Rushen Parish Church. He died in 1986 aged 86.

Captain H. N. KINLEY (40)

Born in 1908 at Port St Mary, he came from a strong seafaring background. His father was a 'Nickey' skipper and Master on coasters. He went to sea in the 1920s with Wilson's of Whitehaven and the Zillah Steamship Co of Liverpool, later becoming Master in Wilson's in his 20s - he was for some time the youngest Master on the British Register. He joined the Steam Packet in 1936 as 2nd Mate of the *Rushen Castle* and in 1939 was the 2nd Mate of the *Mona's Isle* (4). Thereafter he served as relief officer in vessels on war service in the English Channel. He was with the *Viking* during the 1940 evacuations and was on the famous escape of 1,800 children from Guernsey. After the occupation of France, along with most of the Company 2nd Mates, he was laid off but being a holder of a Mersey Pilotage Licence he was seconded to the Liverpool Pilotage Service where he remained for the duration. After hostilities he returned to the Steam Packet as 2nd Mate of the *Viking* and later the *Lady of Mann* (1) for four years. Promoted Mate of the *Peveril* (1) in 1953 he was made Master in 1961.

Master: 1961 to 1973   First Command : *Conister* (1), 1961

He was with the cargo section for four years as Master and was appointed first Master of the new *Peveril* (3) in 1964. His first passenger command was in 1965 on the *King Orry* and thereafter he served on every rung of the passenger ladder to the *Ben-my-Chree* (5) from which he retired in 1973. He was then the Senior Sailing Master of the Fleet. His brother George was also a Steam Packet Master and Commodore 1957 to 1965. His nephew Vernon also became Master, illustrating the strong family traditions within the fleet. Harry Kinley was a fine seaman, ship Master and an experienced ship handler who lived all his Steam Packet career of 37 years in Castletown then retiring to Colby.

After 50 years at sea he enjoyed a long and healthy retirement, lasting until his 95th year in 2003, the longest surviving Steam Packet Master in history? A devout churchman, he was a Church Warden of Arbory Parish and a co-founder of the still most-popular Mariners' Choir.

Captain J. R. KINLEY (42)

Born in Liverpool of Manx parentage in 1916, he was educated in Liverpool and later Douglas. He came from the Kinley dynasty that bore sway in the Steam Packet in the 1930s. His uncle was Marine Superintendent from 1933 to 1956. He went to sea before the war as a seaman with the Steam Packet and British & Irish Steamship Co., obtained his certificates and was an officer in both companies during the war. His first full appointment with the Steam Packet was as 2nd Mate of the *Rushen Castle* in 1946. Thereafter he stepped on all rungs of the ladder until promoted to Chief Officer in 1955 becoming the first Chief Officer on the new *Manx Maid* in 1962.

Master: 1963   First Command: *Conister* (1)

His first passenger command was the *King Orry* (4) in 1968 after which he took his turn, depending on seniority, on all vessels of the fleet of that era. His last appointment was as Master of *Manx Maid*

(2) in season 1974. He was sadly taken ill on the bridge of the *Ben-my-Chree* (5) on 6th March 1975 and died on the same day.

John Richard Kinley was a good seaman and ship Master, an outward-going person and a character, with an unusual mid-Irish Sea drawl. He carried the sobriquet of 'The Rustler' but where that came from, no one was ever quite sure!

175

Captain T. V. KINLEY (54)

Vernon Kinley was born in 1936 and was from Port St Mary. He went to sea as a boy with the scallop fleet and graduated to the Ramsey Steamship Company and then to Coast Lines Liverpool. He acquired Foreign Going Certificates and served with Furness Withy and Cunard as an officer joining the Steam Packet for the 1964 season on the *Manxman* (2). His officer service lasted from 1964 until 1976.

> Master: 1976 to 1998   First Command: *Conister* (2)
> Assistant Marine Superintendent: 1987 to 1998

Thomas Vernon Kinley was an excellent ship Master, a brilliantly clever lad from humble beginnings, acquiring his Foreign Going Certificates and passing his Master's after joining the Steam Packet, the only one at that time to have done so. As a contemporary colleague of the writer's, he was a gentleman and always ready to step in as a relief in emergencies. He was in command on the delivery of the *Peveril* (4), the Company's first ro-ro vessel in 1981. He then saw to the delivery voyage of the unsuccessful *Mona's Isle* (6) from Malta to Glasgow in 1985 and later became the first Steam Packet Master to accept command of a SeaCat in 1994. The highlight of his career was bringing the new *Ben-my-Chree* (6) from Rotterdam on 5th July 1998. He was a fine ship photographer and always had his camera with him on the bridge.

Known to all as Vernon he died in harness suddenly, just days after delivering the 'Ben,' on 21st July 1998.

Captain A. W. G. KISSACK (37)

From Douglas where he was born in 1912, he was educated at the Freemasons' School in London and went to sea as a cadet with Elders & Fyffes of Liverpool. There he obtained all his Foreign-Going Certificates and joined the Steam Packet as a seaman during the depression. He was promoted to 2nd Mate of the *Peel Castle* in 1934 and his officer service lasted until 1956.

> Master: 1957 to 1973   First Command: *Conister* (1)
> First passenger Command: *King Orry* (4), 1962   Fleet Commodore: 1972/ 73
> Assistant Marine Superintendent: 1970   Company Marine Superintendent: 1973 to 1977

In 1939 he was 2nd Mate of the *King Orry* (3) and was in the *Fenella* (2) when she was lost at Dunkirk. Survivors were then transferred to the Thames paddle steamer *Crested Eagle* which was bombed and sank with a heavy loss of life. He managed to swim back to the beaches and was finally rescued by a small craft. Later he was serving with the *Manxman* (1) during the evacuation of Cherbourg and St. Malo where his Captain was Mentioned in Dispatches. He was then seconded to Elders & Fyffes during 1941/ 42 and returned to the Steam Packet in 1943. In 1946 he became the 2nd Mate of the *Lady of Mann* (1) and was promoted to Chief Officer of the *Manx Maid* (1) in the following year. Until going ashore, he served as Master on most of the Company's vessels. He was the first Master of the *Mona's Queen* in 1972 and as Superintendent he oversaw the building of the *Lady of Mann* at Troon in 1976. In retirement he became a Commissioner of Northern Lights and also achieved high honours in Freemasonry. Westby Kissack was a deeply-religious man and later took Holy Orders becoming Curate of St. George's & All Saints. A fine seaman of great experience and a sound shipmate, he was also a good teacher to the younger officers. He enjoyed a quite remarkable career and died aged 78 in 1990.

Captain M. LEADLEY (66)

He was born at Peel in 1950 and came from a seafaring family with a strong fishing background. After Manx schooling at Peel and Douglas, he went to HMS *Indefatigable* Sea Training School in North Wales after which he joined Bank Line of Glasgow for four years. From there he returned to his roots and spent some time fishing before joining the Steam Packet in 1970 as an AB on the *Fenella* (3). He then went for his tickets and rejoined the Company as 2nd Mate in 1973 before moving to the Middle East in 1977.

The foundation of Manx Line in 1978 saw him return to the Island and he was Chief Officer and then Master of the *Manx Viking* until 1985. Following the merger that year he continued in that role, his first Steam Packet command being the *Peveril* (4).

In 1989 he again moved, this time to Belfast Freight Ferries and their *Saga Moon* for a period of ten years. He returned to the Steam Packet for a fourth time in 1999 and is presently a Senior Master of the *Ben-my-Chree* (6).

Captain A. LEE (6)

From Douglas, the first record of him in Steam Packet service was during 1894 as an AB on the paddle steamer *Snaefell* (2). He was promoted to 2nd Mate in 1901 and then to Chief Officer in 1907. In 1912 was Chief Officer of the *Snaefell* (3). During the war he was Chief Officer of the *Empress Queen* until she stranded and was lost on Bembridge Ledge, Isle of Wight in 1916.

Master: 1920   First Command: *Tynwald* (3)

Thereafter he was Master on the *Tynwald* from 1920 until 1926 and then on the *Mona's Isle* (4), *Snaefell* (4), *Viking* and *Manxman*. In 1936 he was on the *Mona's Queen* (3) but he died in harness on 22nd March 1937 aged 68.

The story of his death was passed down to our generation. On his way to join the *Mona's Queen* at Barrow to take her out for Easter 1937, he collapsed and died on the steps of Victoria Pier, apparently in the arms of Captain Crawford Kinley, the Marine Superintendent.

The story was that the *Mona's Queen* (3) was rather a brute to handle with her high superstructure and the prospect of going there added to his stress. From his photo he also had the 30s ship Master trademark of the walrus "tash." By all accounts Arthur Lee was a kindly man and a good ship's Master who was much respected by his subordinates and popular with the travelling public.

Captain M. MAUGHAN (44)

Mathew Maughan was born in 1910 at Wylam, Northumberland but his family moved to the Isle of Man in 1918 for his education. On leaving school at 15 he was apprenticed to a Liverpool shipping company where he served his seagoing trade. On completing his cadetship, he served with Ellermans of Liverpool as an officer, then during the war with Silver Line where he served in all the theatres of war, even being torpedoed and sunk twice. He joined the Steam Packet in 1947 as 2nd Mate serving for a considerable time on the *Manxman* (1) then sailing on Ministry of War Transport duties from Harwich to the Hook of Holland until 1949, when that vessel was handed back to the Company and scrapped. Officer service: 1947 to 1965. Promoted Chief Officer: 1958

Master: 1965 to 1974   First Command: *Ramsey*, 1965

He was Master of the *King Orry* (4) in 1968 and 1969. Thereafter he remained on the cargo vessel *Peveril* (3) from 1970 to 1974 until his natural retirement in January 1975. A quiet, fine-looking man, a competent seaman and ship Master, Mattie Maughan had but a very short retirement, passing away in April 1975.

Captain W. E. McMEIKEN (33)

A native of Peel where he was born in 1907, he went to sea as a boy with the herring fleet and then with local, foreign and national coasting companies as a seaman, joining the Steam Packet as a seaman in 1928. He obtained his tickets and was promoted to 2nd Mate in 1932, becoming Chief Officer two years later.

Master: 1948 to 1972   First Command: *Conister* (1)   **Commodore: 1970 to 1972**

In 1939 he was Chief Officer of the *Snaefell* (4) and during war he took part in the Dunkirk evacuation and Normandy Landings and other hostilities wherever required. In 1946 he became Chief Officer on the *Ben-my-Chree* (4). He was promoted to Master in 1948 but with the sale of the *Manxman* (1) in 1949 reverted back to Mate for three years on the *Lady of Mann* (1). From 1952 he was promoted to Master permanently and served on every rung of the ladder in command, his last two years on the *Ben-my-Chree* (5) as Commodore.

William Ernest McMeiken was familiarly known as 'Ernie Mac', although like most of his colleagues he acquired by-names along the way and one which he carried throughout his career was "Hurricane Hutch" because of a particular bad winter he had on the *Conister* (1). An extremely competent seaman, an excellent ship Master and handler in the best traditions of a Manx seaman, he was a strict disciplinarian and woe betide anyone who transgressed. He retired in 1972 and was one of the founders of the Mariners' Choir, working hard to make it the success it became. He died in 1989 aged 82.

Captain B. H. MOORE (51)

Brian Moore was born in Wallasey in 1928. His father was a Master and Superintendent with the Kuwait Oil Company. He went to sea straight from school as a cadet with the British Tanker Company. He sailed there as 3rd Mate in his last year of apprenticeship and obtained all his Foreign Going and Master's Certificates by the age of 26. He was then Chief Officer and Master on the tankers of the Standard Vacuum Oil Company. After 18 years Foreign Going, he joined the Steam Packet in 1962 as 2nd Mate on the *Mona's Isle* (5) and moved to the Isle of Man to be near his family. He was promoted to Chief Officer in 1964.

Master: 1974   First Command: *Ramsey*

Captain Moore was thereafter Master on each step of the ladder including relieving on all vessels until 1978, when he became ill. His final appointment was on the *Manxman* (2) but his last actual duty was as Master of the *Mona's Queen* (5). Brian Moore died in harness in 1979 aged 51. He was indeed a fine man in all senses and an exceptional seaman. He adapted well into the fleet and took his turn like the rest of us. His premature passing was a shock to us all. He acquitted himself with distinction in what was a second career, was well regarded by the Management, looked on with affection by his peers and respected by both crews and the travelling public alike.

Captain R. J. MOORE (64)

He was born in 1947 at Port St. Mary and as a young man worked in the local fishing fleet before his apprenticeship with Alfred Holt's Blue Funnel Line from 1965 to 1971. He then joined the United Baltic Corporation in 1972 after which he obtained his Master's Foreign Going Certificate at Hull in 1976. It was then to Ocean Inchcape supply vessels where he achieved his first command in 1978. He joined Manx Line as Chief Officer in the following year and after the 1985 merger continued in the role until becoming Master in 1992. His first command was the *King Orry* (5) and he continues to serve as Master of the *Ben-my-Chree* (6) today. Roger Moore is a fine, upstanding Manxman and a competent seaman who is popular with the passengers. He enjoys the respect of his crews and is worthy of the command he holds.

Captain T. G. MOORE (71)

Captain Moore is from Morecambe in Lancashire where he was born in 1965. He first went to sea during 1983 with Caledonian MacBrayne on their Western Isles routes. From there he obtained his Certificates and attained his Class One Master Mariner's in 1997. He then served for a time as a watch keeping officer with P & O and came to the Steam Packet in 1999 as Chief Officer of the *Ben-my-Chree*. (6).

He was promoted Master of the *SeaCat Isle of Man* in July 2001 and since then has sailed as Master during the summer months both on the SeaCat while also taking his turn on the *Ben-my-Chree*. Terry Moore is another recent addition to our number and having taken the responsibility of command is fully entitled to his place on our roll of honour. A highly qualified and competent young man, he is a worthy successor to his predecessors.

With such young men coming to the fore, the travelling public can be assured that they are in good hands and the Company's future is well secured.

Captain D. O'TOOLE (67)

Born in 1949 at Derbyhaven, he was educated at Castle Rushen High School before moving to the *Indefatigable* Sea Training School for 18 months. He then served his apprenticeship with London & Overseas Freighters Ltd becoming 3rd and then 2nd Officer before joining Manchester Liners in 1973 as 2nd and Chief Officer. In 1976 he joined the Ocean Weather Service and after a further two years joined the Steam Packet as 2nd Mate in May 1978. The following year he moved to the new Manx Line and resumed his Steam Packet career after the merger of 1985. He was promoted to Master in 1997 and his first command was the *SeaCat Isle of Man*. Since then he has served as Master on all the present fleet.

Dermot O'Toole is a much-experienced seaman and officer who has honed those skills to hold a command most competently. He is one of three brothers all of whom are officers with the Steam Packet.

It is such family traditions that have served the Steam Packet and the Isle of Man so well and is further testimony of the 175 years of service to the Island.

Captain G. PETERS (61)

Born in Liverpool of Welsh stock in 1944, he served his time as a cadet with Alfred Holt - Blue Funnel - and sailed there as a watchkeeping officer. He joined the Steam Packet in 1972 as 2nd Mate, later being promoted to Chief Officer. His Steam Packet officer service lasted 20 years.

> Master: 1991   First Command: *Peveril* (4)

Thereafter he served on whatever ship was required and was one of the first Masters of the new *Ben-my-Chree*. Gwyn Peters lived at Criccieth, North Wales and remained there during his Steam Packet career. He was therefore the first Steam Packet Master not to reside on the Island. He was a natural seaman and a good ship-mate.

Captain W. QUALTROUGH (12)

Born in Birkenhead in 1877 where his father worked in the shipyard, he grew up in Ballasalla to where his family returned and his father worked for the railway. He went to sea as a boy in the herring fleet and then served coastwise as a seaman. He then went foreign-going before joining the Steam Packet before the First War. The first record of him as an officer was as 2nd Mate in the *Mona* (4) during 1919.

> Master: 1928 to 1945   First Command: *Mona* (4)

He was the first Master of the new *Peveril* (2) in 1929 and then worked in a variety of ships until made Master of the new *Fenella* (2) in 1937, a role in which he continued until 1940. Thereafter he served when and where required but declining health towards the end of his working life saw him on Pier Duty at Douglas for a long spell.

Wilfred Qualtrough (known as 'Wilfie') retired towards the end of 1945 at the cessation of hostilities. He died in 1953 at the age of 76.

Captain T. QUAYLE (9)

From Castletown - he was born in 1872. His first record of Steam Packet service was as a seaman in 1892. He was promoted to 2nd Mate in 1900 and to Chief Officer in 1912. During the First War he was Chief Officer on the *Tynwald* (3) when she took on survivors of the American liner *New York* which had been torpedoed at the Mersey Bar. Passengers included Admiral Sims of the US Navy and all were landed at Liverpool.

Master: 1925   First Command: *Fenella* (1)

He was Master of the *Peel Castle* for three years, then the *Rushen Castle* in 1932 and the *Mona's Isle* (4) in 1933. From what information the writer has of him, he was called Thomas but had the nickname of "The Whallag". It is assumed that this name is derived from the small croft whence he came, which lay on the slopes of South Barrule, the ruins of which can still be found on the banks of Cringle Reservoir in the Parish of Malew. He must have been a good-living and gentle man, and was reputed to be rather nervous because singing hymns on the bridge, when things were tense, was the order of the day. (That story passed down from Capt.'Ginger' Bridson.). Like all his colleagues he sported a fine 'tash'. He died on 19th April 1934, aged 62 and is buried at Malew.

175

Captain H. QUINE (3)

Born in 1865 in Port St Mary. The first mention we have of him was as a seaman on the *Ellan Vannin* during 1886. He was promoted to 2nd Mate in 1893 and to Chief Officer in 1901.

Master: 1911   First Command: *Fenella* (1)   Commodore: 1933 to 1936

In 1912 he commanded the paddle steamer *King Orry* (2): During the 1914-1918 War he served as Master on the *Tynwald* (3). Then between 1920- 1926, he was in the *King Orry* (3) and in 1927 on the *Manxman* which was then the 'No 2' ship. Capt. Quine served on the *Ben-my-Chree* (4) from 1933 to 1936 during which time he was the Fleet Commodore.
From this length in time, not a lot can be said of him. His name was Henry but he was more popularly known as 'Hal'. As was common during that era he worked on past the age of 70 and was known for his flowing walrus 'tashes giving him, and many others of that time, a similar look. By all accounts he was a fine man – he certainly looked the part and was a good seaman, ship Master and was well respected by all.
He retired in Spring 1936, aged 71.

Captain J. B. QUIRK (46)

From Douglas where he was born in 1934, he went to sea as a cadet with Hogarth's of Ardrossan/ Glasgow, acquiring his Foreign Going Certificates and sailing with the company as an Officer. He joined the Steam Packet in 1957. His officer service lasted from 1957 to 1967,

**Master: 1968 to 1989   First Command: *Ramsey*   Assistant Marine Superintendent: 1977
Commodore: 1987 to 1989**

On every step of the ladder on his way up, John Bernard Quirk was an excellent ship Master and handler and was always his own man. He was Senior Master of the *Mona's Queen* (5) for 12 years. As Assistant Superintendent he oversaw the entry into the fleet of the *Peveril* (4) and *Tynwald* (6) which was his last command. He was known to one and all as 'Bernie'. He retired on medical grounds in 1989.

Captain J. E. QUIRK (30)

From Bradda, Port Erin, he was born in 1904. He came from a seafaring background; his father, Captain J.J. Quirk, had been a Master with the Steam Packet and his Kinley uncles likewise. On leaving school he went to sea in the coastwise trade in various companies and also as a seaman with the Steam Packet. He was Master with John Stewart's of Glasgow in 1932 and joined the Steam Packet the following year as Mate on the death of his father.

> Officer Service: 1933 to 1945   Master: 1946 to 1969   First Command: *Peveril* (2)
> Fleet Commodore: 1965 to 1969

He was Chief Officer of the *Fenella* (2) in the 1939 season and when she was sunk at Dunkirk on 29th May 1940. He was also on ps *Crested Eagle* when she too was sunk with much loss of life. By the time of D-Day he was Chief Officer of the *Victoria*. After the war he became Master on most of the Company's vessels, beginning with the *Rushen Castle*, and in 1962 brought out the first new car ferry *Manx Maid* (2) followed by the new *Ben-my-Chree* in 1966. He was Commodore for four years before retiring in January 1969. He was a most competent Master, ship handler and an agreeable shipmate. His Christian name was Edward but he was always referred to as 'Eddie'. He died aged 78 in 1982.

Captain J. E. RONAN (48)

Born at Glenchass Farm at Port St. Mary in 1929; as there was heavy snow at the time, the midwife couldn't get through and so his father had to 'do the honours'. His education was limited to the Four Roads Central School from 1934 to 1943. Prior to going to sea he worked in the bakehouse - hence the early name of "Baker". He was a member of the Army Cadet Force and Home Guard before going to sea as a boy rating via the training ship *Vindicatrix* in September 1945.

He came from a family with long nautical associations with the Steam Packet and seafaring in general and his service with the Company lasted from 1945 to 1989. He served as a rating in the period 1945 to 1957 and during this time alternated between the Steam Packet Company, foreign-going and coastwise vessels as this was the accepted pattern of things in the early and mid 20th century. He served as a seaman and officer with John Stewarts of Glasgow, periodically from 1951 to 1957, and it was during this period that he met and married his Scottish lassie, Lizzie Lang of Grangemouth. His service as a Steam Packet officer lasted from 1958 until 1969.

> Master: 1969 to 1986   First Command: *Ramsey*, 1970

Captain Ronan served as an officer and Master on all of the company's vessels in his generation. He was Master of the *Ben-my-Chree* (5) from 1973 to 1984 and the appointed Senior Master from 1977 to 1984. He was the Senior Sailing Master (after Commodore) from 1977 and his last command was the *Tynwald* (6). He lived in Castletown for most of his Steam Packet career and in retirement he accepted a position as Relief Officer with the IOM Fishery Patrol on mpv *Enbarr* for seven years He also resumed the ancient nautical hobby of rope mat making - a nostalgic reminder of the days before the mast - and is still taking orders!

Captain S. M. SPENSER (70)

From Douglas where he was born in 1970. He was educated at Murray's Road School and then Ballakermeen and St Ninian's High Schools. His path to the sea was a traditional Manx one in the 20th century. From school he went straight to work as a junior rating on the *Lady of Mann* (2) in 1986 and the *Mona's Queen* (5) in 1987. He then went foreign-going with Shell Tankers for seven years which took him world-wide. With encouragement from Alan Chivers of Shell Marine personnel, he studied for his 2nd Mate's ticket which was successfully obtained. Returning to Shell for a couple of trips he then came to the Steam Packet as a summer relief, serving with the United Baltic Corporation in the winter sailing around Europe. He returned to the Steam Packet in 1995 as a permanent officer and gained his Foreign Master's Certificate in 2002.

> Master: 2002   First Command: *SeaCat Isle of Man* then *Lady of Mann* in the same year

Stephen Spenser was also in charge of the *Lady of Mann* during her charter in the Azores in summers 2002, 2003 and 2004. He is another young seaman continuing the long tradition of Manxmen going down to the sea and manning our Island Lifeline.

Captain W. SQUIRES (20)

Born in 1883 at Port St Mary, his father Cornelius was a schoolmaster who taught navigation. One of a large family, at the age of 15 he went to sea in the fishing fleet on the 'Nickie' *Celestine*. From there he served on Home Trade vessels until joining the Steam Packet in the early part of the 20th century. He served with the fleet and is recorded as being lamp trimmer on the *Peel Castle* and then Mate on *Tyrconnel* in the 1920s.

Master: 1929   First Command: *Cushag*

Although not the holder of a Master's ticket, he was given command because of his great experience of Home Trade waters. His first trip was in 1929 with a cargo of coal to Ireland and he continued as Master of the *Cushag* from 1929 until 1943. A religious man, he did not work on the Sabbath; he spent most Sundays preaching in country chapels in the south of the Island.

Wallace Squires, while not the holder of the necessary certificates, acquitted himself with distinction throughout his career and served the Company well. He had the reputation of being a kindly man, and the photo amply illustrates that virtue. When the *Cushag* came to the southern "outports" there was always a boatload of locals and children going for a trip through the Calf Sound to Peel.

When the *Cushag* was sold in 1943 he moved to become Mate of the *Conister* (1) until his death in harness in 1947. He died aged 64 at his home in Douglas but prior to remarrying had lived most of his working life in Castletown.

Captain O. TAYLOR (21)

From Port St Mary where he was born in 1892. He was with the Steam Packet as a seaman before the First War and also had other coastal and foreign-going shipping experience. The first record as a Steam Packet Officer was as 2nd Mate in 1921. He became Chief Officer in 1928.

Master: 1934 to 1957.   First Command: *Conister* (1)

In 1939 he was Master on the *Mona's Isle* (4) and during the war he served wherever required. After the war his appointed ship was the *Manxman* (1) which was then still under Ministry of War Transport control at Dover and Harwich carrying troops, returning German prisoners of war and carrying displaced people and where the writer served under him. In 1947 he brought out the new *Tynwald* before returning to the *Manxman* at Harwich. Due to some refusal to go there, he lost two places in seniority in 1948.

Oscar Taylor was an unassuming man of slight stature, a fine seaman of the "old school" and an excellent ship Master. He retired in 1957 from the new *Manxman* (2) and died aged 80 in 1972.

Captain W. WATSON (8)

From Peel where he was born in c1877, the first mention we have of him in Steam Packet service was in 1912 as 2nd Mate of the *Queen Victoria*. He was promoted to Chief Officer of the *Prince of Wales* in 1914 and saw service with the RNR during the First War.

Master: 1920   First Command: *Douglas* (3)

Captain Watson was Master of the unfortunate *Douglas* when she was sunk in collision in the Mersey in 1923. Being non-culpable he was able to resume his career and was Master on most of the vessels of the era: *Fenella*, *Mona* (1927), ps *Mona's Queen* 1928, *Rushen Castle* 1930, *Ramsey Town* 1931/32, *Snaefell* 1933, *Viking* 1934 and *Manxman* 1935/36.

In 1937 he achieved command on the new *Mona's Queen* (3). On 23rd August 1937, taking the Harland & Wolff excursion from Liverpool, at home between trips at Douglas he died most suddenly, thus ending a rather colourful life and further giving the *Mona's Queen* (3) the reputation as a widow maker! I have especially included Capt. Watson in the 1930s roll of honour as there seem to have been so many stories of the man passed down from our previous generation. Of a strong character and a reputed stentorian voice, he spent his early seagoing years trading on the American seaboard and consequently had picked up an American 'drawl.' When a 'yarn' was to be told, it came out with no uncertain flourish. The favourite story told many times courtesy of Capt. Lyndhurst Callow - and others - concerned a 'terrier' called "Rough on Rats" who was apparently another great character. At New York on a run ashore "Rough" went missing and they had to leave without him. On reaching Buenos Aires many days later, who was on the quayside waiting for them but old "Rough" who had been carried down by a liner

175

who knew of his ship. Apparently he did not stray again!

Another story was recalled many times. At the enquiry after the sinking of the *Douglas* he was asked if he had anything to say to which he replied, "Learned gentlemen, I have listened to your findings and what it has taken you two weeks to deliberate upon - I only had 30 seconds."

The third story is of his encounters with Mr. John Hallsall, the Company's Marine Superintendent of those days. Mr. Hallsall was not a seaman as such but a ship's carpenter - a position which the Company held in much esteem in those days and carried much authority. In spite of this, he was still the boss.

Captain Watson was a man of high nautical qualifications and experience and did not have a great regard for Mr. Hallsall's unqualified standing. He frequently would hail him as the ship pulled away, "Get back to making five-barred gates, Hallsall!"

This was very much appreciated by the junior officers, to whom Hallsall apparently gave a hard life. Captain Watson was a much respected and revered Steam Packet Master and would only be around 60 years of age when he died.

Captain A. WHITEWAY (18)

From Douglas where he was born in 1888. His family came from a Liverpool fishing background. He first joined the Steam Packet as a seaman in 1908 and after war service in the Royal Navy rejoined the Company being promoted to 2nd Mate of the *Mona* (4) in1920 and seeing officer service from 1920 until 1934. He served as Chief Officer from 1925 until 1933.

Master: 1934 to 1953   First Command: *Mona* (4)

At the outbreak of war in 1939 he was Master of the *Snaefell* (4) and later served wherever required. After the war he brought out the new *King Orry* in 1946 followed by the new *Snaefell* in 1948 and the new *Mona's Isle* in 1951. Bringing out three new ships in six years is a record for any Master in the Steam Packet. He was the first Master the writer served under and was always an inspiration. Albert Whiteway was a seaman of the old school and looked the part, being an excellent ship Master and handler and a worthy example to all those who followed.

His brother, John Henry Whiteway, also served with the Company as Chief Officer and was Master for a time at Dunkirk. In 1953 Captain A. Whiteway retired from his new *Mona's Isle*. Always a person to keep his attachment with things nautical, he made rope mats in retirement. He died in 1964 aged 75.

Captain J. H. WHITEWAY, DSC (27)

From Douglas, a brother of Captain Albert Whiteway, he came from a Liverpool fishing family and joined the Steam Packet as 2nd Mate in the early 1920s. He was made Chief Officer in 1928 and was the first Chief Officer of the new *Tynwald* in 1937 until the war. He had sailed as relief Master in the 1930's. As Master of the *Tynwald* at Dunkirk, he made four trips and took out 9,000 troops and was indeed the last vessel to leave during Operation Dynamo with 3,000 souls on board. For his heroism and dedication to the cause he was awarded the Distinguished Service Cross. Thereafter during the war he served wherever required and was for some time on the Home Station running to Fleetwood, from where this photo was presented. He retired in 1945 and died in 1958.

Captain N. WILD (63)

From Peel but he was born at Thornton Heath in Surrey in 1947. His family came to the IOM and he was educated on the Island at The Dhoon, The Peel Clothworkers' and Douglas High Schools. This was followed by an academic period at the University of Wales, Swansea where he obtained a Bachelor of Science degree in Zoology and afterwards a Post Graduate Certificate in Education. He taught in schools on the Island for two years then worked in the Marine Biological Station at Port Erin researching seaweeds. It was there that the call of the sea beckoned and he took a job as a deck hand in the *Vingafjord*, a vessel out of Peel running foodstuffs into the Island from Northern Ireland ports. In time he took a seaman's position with the Steam Packet on the *Fenella* (3) and later on the passenger ships. After completing his qualifying sea time, he went to the Fleetwood Nautical College and came back with a Mate's ticket. Thus he began a new career and was 2nd Mate for three years and Chief Officer for ten.

Master: 1989   First Command: *Peveril* (4)

He served mostly in the cargo section but also took command of the passenger vessels *Tynwald* (6) and *King Orry* (5), as and when required. Nigel Wild did not come into the trade by the usual and accepted traditional paths but he held his own as a seaman, officer and ship's Master. In 1995 because of domestic arrangements he decided to swallow the anchor and went ashore to keep a pub in Lancashire. At the time of writing he now has a guest house on the Isle of Arran. He was an extremely talented scholar who became a fine seaman with a nice outward personality and was most popular with passengers and colleagues alike.

Captain G. WOODS (11)

Captain Woods was from Castletown and served with the Steam Packet from before the First War period being promoted to Chief Officer in 1920 on the *Mona's Isle* (4) during her first year with the Company. He was later promoted to Acting Master in 1928 on the *Rushen Castle* during Captain Comish's illness.

Master: 1929   First Command: *Mona* (4)   Commodore: 1939 to 1940

He was Master throughout the 1930s on the senior vessels,1937/38 on the new *Fenella* (2) and *Mona's Queen* (3) and in 1939 he was Master of the *Ben-my-Chree* (4) which carried his Commodore's flag. During the Dunkirk evacuation he twice took the 'Ben' into that cauldron. George Woods retired shortly after this experience and is remembered in Castletown as the benefactor who gave land for the local football club to have its own ground. The photo was taken on the 'Ben' c1939. He died in 1952.

Captain J. WOODS (59)

Born in 1940 in Douglas and educated at King William's College, he later went to sea as a cadet with British India. He joined the Steam Packet in 1968 as 2nd Mate and was promoted to Chief Officer in 1970. He later left the Company to join Esso in 1974.

First Command: *Manx Viking*, 1978   First Steam Packet Command: *Tynwald* (6)

He joined the new Manx Line in 1978 as Master and remained there until the merger of 1985. He then served on whatever ship was required of him until retirement in 1999.

Captain T. C. WOODS, OBE (10)

He was born in 1879 at Port St Mary. Like so many of his generation, Captain Woods started his working life and seagoing career as a boy in the 1890s herring fleet. He then went to sea in sailing vessels and qualified for his Master's Foreign Going Sailing Ship (Square Rigged) Certificate, the last such ever in Steam Packet service. His early records are obscure now but it is known he had joined the Steam Packet as a seaman as long ago as 1897. The first record of him as a Steam Packet officer is just after the First War.

Master: 1927 to 1946   First record of Command: *Tynwald* (3) in 1927
Commodore: 1940 to 1946, probably the most momentous years of the Company history.
He carried his flag in the *Lady of Mann* (1)

He was in command of the *Lady of Mann* from 1937 until 1946 taking part in the evacuation of Dunkirk where he took the ship on three occasions bringing out 4,260 troops, for this action he was Mentioned in Dispatches. Later he also worked along the western French ports of Le Havre (from where he left with 5,000 troops on board), Cherbourg and then Brest. Thereafter from 1940 to 1944 the ship was engaged on active trooping assignments in northern waters and delegated as a tender to the Cunard 'Queens' at Belfast Lough and Tail of the Bank.
At D-Day the 'Lady' carried Canadian assault troops to land on Juno Beach. Thomas Corris Woods - known as Tom - was a fine seaman who was very much of the "old school" and looked the part. Remembered as a quiet kindly man with a twinkle in his eye and also known as 'Daddy' which explains an awful lot.
A story about Captain Woods, and related by Captain Louis Bridson, concerns the time when the 'Lady' was carrying a full complement of soldiers out of Brest. Following the sinking of the Cunard liner *Lancastria*, which was about to sail when she had a bomb dropped down her funnel, the sea was full of struggling men. Tom stopped his ship to pick up survivors even though his destroyer escort ordered him to leave them where they were. The writer saw him bring the *Lady of Mann* into Douglas Harbour on 9th March 1946, on her return after war service to a civic reception, his last active duty before retirement. He remarked at the time he had taken her away in 1939 and brought her back in one piece which even from this distance in time has to be recognised as a superb achievement. For his outstanding war service and being the Company Senior Master he was awarded the OBE. He had a well-deserved retirement of some 25 years and died in 1971 aged 91. Tom Woods was surely a Manx seaman of the highest order.

the officers & crews

175

CHAPTER TWELVE

The Officers & Crews
by Captain Jack Ronan

The boys have left the village the season has begun
The boys have left the village the Packet boats to run

So went the ditty one would hear bandying around the fo'c'sles. There were other terse lines one would hear repeated but no others were quite so apt. However, this clearly demonstrated the relationship between the Island's rural people and the Company whose ships carried all that humanity over the many years; from the mill towns of Lancashire, the banks of the Clyde and many other such places in northern Britain, the very lifeblood of the Manx economy for over a century and a half.

The year 1938 was probably the apex of our tourist industry when the Steam Packet had a fleet of eighteen ships. Fifteen of those were passenger vessels with an average crew of 60 although there were even more on the labour-intensive coal burners, which would mean an overall floating staff of say 900. Add to that the shore and office staff and the Company at the height of those seasons would have some 1,500 souls on the payroll. I am also including the staff at Liverpool and other outports to illustrate the immense operation serving such a relatively small Island. All hands were able-bodied adults and as an analogy could be classed the population of a small town or large village. The workforce as a whole was indeed labour intensive on a grand scale!

Of the floating staff, it would be fair to say the majority of them came from the Island's fishing towns and country villages, some were even from the remotest hill districts who answered the call of the sea to make an honest living. Some would aspire to greater responsibility while others, and this would be the bulk of them, were happy to remain in their respective fo'c'sles. We also must not forget the occasional lady who helped "man" the fleet and until recent times they would only be employed in the Catering Department but they had a story to tell in their own right! Today there are also most competent female Navigational Officers.

While remembering in principle the overall Manxness of the crewing and the whole operation, I have to acknowledge and concede that there were also many who came from the adjacent Islands, from the ports of Barrow and Liverpool/ Birkenhead where the ships laid up for the long winters and who also played such a part of this infinite story. Without them the ships could not have operated.

Due to the bond that prevailed between these men of the sea and because of their mostly Island backgrounds, a strong

Tynwald 1939
Eddie Quirk, Chief Officer, Captain Jack Keig and Alan Watterson, 2nd Officer.

community spirit and camaraderie existed that transcended rank and department, which is amply illustrated in the content of the accompanying photographs.

Family and friendship ties abounded – and still do - it was not uncommon for the Captain to have a brother in the stokehold firing coal and a Chief Engineer to have a brother as a sailor in the seamen's fo'c'sle. There were also many uncles-nephews and close cousins with similar bonds throughout the fleet. However, each and every one did recognise rank and seniority and the same code of conduct and discipline that existed throughout the entire Merchant Service was respected in the Steam Packet as elsewhere. From my own experience I would say it was probably more relaxed but that apart, it was woe betide anyone who wantonly transgressed although this was not often as holding on to their jobs was paramount.

Until recent times the men who came from the fishing and country backgrounds held strong religious beliefs, were God-fearing and church-going. This attitude and belief complemented the respect held for authority and the charge with which they were entrusted.

Victoria 1929

Tommy Barlow   James Watterson   Jack Kelso   Louis Merrifield

Jimmy Reader   Nelson Brown   Ernest McMeiken   Bill Postlethwaite   Jack Blundell

Willie Cowell   Cecil Canipa   J H Whiteway   Captain. Jack Morrison   T L Corkill   Jack Cain   Tom Hudson

Tynwald 1928

Back Row: Firemen/Greasers, on left: W A Cubbon, Surby, Sailor with luggage: Tommy Barlow, Next: Willie Kavra, Cregneish, Extreme right: Tom Kelly, The Howe,
Sailor with Cup: Bob McDonald, Peel
Chief Officer: George Kinley, Master 1937-65, Commodore 1958-65, Captain: J J Quirk, Bradda, Port Erin, Chief Engineer: Jim Beckerley, Douglas/Barrow

Snaefell 1938

Fox   T Gelling   J Kelly   A Corkish   J Moore

Jim Beckerley   Captain Archie Holkham   Ernest McMeiken   Cecil Canepa

At South Edward Pier, Douglas, August 1938

Captain C A Kinley, Skipper of the tug **Ganges**   Captain. J E Quirk   Captain. R Clucas Jnr.

Photo by IOM Times to commemorate the departure of the **Rushen Castle** for scrapping at Ghent (January 1947)

Lady of Mann *1951*

| *Arthur Costain* | *Cecil Kenna* | *Captain P B Cowley* | *W E McMeiken* | *H N Kinley* | *Ted Daugherty* |
| *2nd Engineer* | *Chief Engineer* | *Master* | *Chief Officer* | *2nd Officer* | *Purser* |

(Photo by IOM Examiner: Lady's 21st Anniversary)

The Mayor's Parlour, Douglas, 20th October 1962

(Manx Press Pictures, Prospect Hill, Douglas)

The **Manx Maid's** *First Sailing 1962*

James B Garside   *Captain Eddie Quirk*
Chairman

Captain W E McMeiken's Retirement, March 1972

| *Derek Minshall* | *Rev. R Evans* | *George Johnson* | *Ernie McMeiken* | *Chaplain* |
| *Chief Engineer* | *Missions to Seamen* | *Chief Steward* | *Captain* | *Liverpool* |

Manx Maid *at Liverpool Landing Stage*

Fleetwood 1956   The **Mona's Queen**
Visit to the Mayor's Parlour to commemorate the opening of Summer Service.
Captain J E Quirk, Captain C Banyard, Chief Officer James Cannon behind Chief Engineer Cyril Watterson

Manx Maid *1963*

K Bridson (Ken)   *Captain J E Quirk (Eddie)*   *Chief Officer J S Kennaugh (John)*

131

*Douglas harbour in July 1982 with the freight vessel **nf Jaguar** and the **Manx Maid** at the King Edward VIII Pier and the **Mona's Queen** at the Victoria Pier.*
(John Hendy)

steam packet day

CHAPTER THIRTEEN

Steam Packet Day

by Captain Peter Corrin

ON THIS DAY – Captain Peter Corrin recounts a typical Steam Packet day

On this day 30th June 2004 (the 174th anniversary of the launching of the *Mona's Isle* in 1830) - dawn over Douglas is overcast with a moderate-to-fresh south-westerly wind as recorded in the voyage log of the Ben-my-Chree. At 06.01, under the command of Captain Steve Cowin, she berths safely on No. 5 berth (North Edward Pier) and in so doing completes her 587th voyage of 2004. Her payload on this voyage consists of 18 passengers, six cars, one motorcycle and approximately 650 metres of freight.

The relatively low passenger figure is due to the fact that one sailing a week in each direction to and from Heysham is dedicated to the carriage of dangerous goods essential for the Island's business and the hospital in particular. On these occasions there is a maximum passenger allowance of 41 and because she was in dock for her biennial overhaul earlier in the year, she will perform over 1,300 voyages during 2004. In the intermediate years this will exceed 1,400.

This demonstrates the multi-functional aspect of the *Ben-my-Chree*, which is in stark contrast to 1970, my first season as Second Officer in a passenger vessel on the 1948-built *Snaefell* (5) at a time when the Company operated eight passenger and three cargo vessels. Like most of her 'sisters,' the *Snaefell* operated between May and September with the year-round operation being conducted by the car ferries *Ben-my-Chree* (5) and *Manx Maid* (2).

The *Snaefell* completed 200 sailings that season so it is no exaggeration to say that the current *Ben-my-Chree* is doing the work of at least seven ships of nearly 35 years ago.

A flurry of tugmasters buzzing to and fro like bees discharge the vessel, ensuring all the major stores have their perishables available on the shelves and the Island's population their newspapers to peruse over breakfast.

Across the harbour at No. 1 berth Victoria Pier, the *SeaCat Isle of Man* has commenced her embarkation of passengers (comprising both business people and many day-excursionists) and vehicles under the watchful eye of First Officer Laurie Royston in preparation for her morning departure to Liverpool. Laurie is the Company's first female Deck Officer and demonstrates its commitment to equal opportunities. The check-in staff and Duty Official working in harmony with the ship's staff have done a good job and loading has been smooth and uneventful. Consequently, at

*Captain Peter Corrin on board the **Lady of Mann** (2).* (Miles Cowsill)

06.55, some five minutes ahead of schedule, Captain Dominic Bell gives the instruction to 'let go fore and aft' and she backs away from her berth, swings in the harbour and proceeds on course for Liverpool.

Exactly one hour later, at 07.55, the *SuperSeaCat Two* departs Liverpool on her sailing to Dublin. The route has been serviced by several operators and vessels in the past including the *Lady of Mann* until 1998 when the *SuperSeaCat Two* made her debut providing a city centre-to-city centre route of approximately four hours' duration. She will be leaving the Mersey at Q1 as the *SeaCat Isle of Man* approaches the Bar Light, whilst over in Douglas the final figures are being despatched to the *Ben-my-Chree* ahead of her departure to Heysham. The final figures consist of the

The **SeaCat Isle of Man** is seen arriving at Douglas during her last season on the Irish Sea for the Company. The vessel was originally built as **Hoverspeed France** and proved to be a very reliable craft for the Company. (Miles Cowsill)

An early morning scene at Douglas harbour with the unloading of the **Ben-my-Chree** following her arrival from Heysham. The vessel provides a vital link for the everyday needs of the Island, including the transportation of the daily newspapers. (IOMSP Co Ltd)

total numbers of passengers, vehicles and freight and are necessary to complete the stability programme prior to the vessel's departure. She is now under the command of Captain Colin Duggan whose grandfather was also a Master in the Company and had a distinguished career not least during the war years.

The Steam Packet has in many ways been a 'family affair' over the years with long lines of dynasties running through it. Perhaps the most well-known were the 'Kinley's' – a line which was sadly broken with the untimely death in 1998 of my colleague Vernon, who as mentor and friend had such a major influence on my career with the Company.

My normal routine, like many others, is to arrive at the office in Imperial Buildings and, after checking overnight mail, proceed onto the *Ben-my-Chree* to discuss any general matters with the Master and Chief Officer. It would be usual at this point to meet the Managing Director, Hamish Ross, who would be talking to several crew members as well as mingling with the passengers for some first-hand feedback.

Back in the office I would meet other colleagues and in particular Mark Woodward (Operations Director), Geoff Corkish (Communications Manager), Frank O'Neill (Technical Manager) and Sean Orton (Freight Manager), at which point a general discussion would take place on any overnight issues ashore or afloat. Almost before we had settled into our office routine, the *SeaCat Isle of Man* had transited the Mersey and even allowing for reducing speed from C23 buoy to comply with port regulations was 'all fast' at the Landing Stage at 09.39.

Throughout my tenure of office, perhaps the most significant change has been the introduction of fast craft. In November 1990 when the *Hoverspeed Great Britain* came to the Isle of Man for a promotional visit, I considered it a privilege to be asked to sail on her from Portsmouth and to be the local pilot for her arrival in Douglas. Our route was via Falmouth and Pembroke Dock. Her arrival in Douglas was greeted by a large number of people and attracted a huge amount of interest. There was no doubt her

appearance over the horizon heralded the dawn of a new era in Manx shipping history and for me it was good to be part of it.

There is a saying in Manx Gaelic called 'Traa Dy Liooar' which means 'time enough', but speed is of the essence in getting to and from the Island and since the introduction of fast craft on a regular basis in 1994 they have proved enormously successful. Tradition though still plays a major part in the Company's strategy and some 1,415 miles from Liverpool, perhaps the epitome of that tradition - the *Lady of Mann* - is preparing to sail from Ponta Delgada to Santa Maria on what has become a regular voyage during her annual charter operating in the Azores. Under the command of Captain Allan Albiston, who shares the role with Captain Steve Spenser, she will sail throughout the archipelago for the next twelve weeks, returning to Irish Sea services in October. It would have been hard to imagine when Captain John Kennaugh took her on her maiden voyage to Liverpool on exactly that day in 1976 that she would be celebrating its 28th anniversary so far from her native shores. However, it demonstrates very much the flexibility of her design as she could actually have been built for the ports in the Azores, which in many cases mirror some of those in the Isle of Man. It is also indicative of the Company policy to seek business opportunities well outside its usual operating area.

After an uneventful voyage, although in unseasonably strong SSW winds, the *Ben-my-Chree* arrives in Heysham at 12.35. Despite these conditions, the *SeaCat Isle of Man* arrives back in Douglas on schedule at 13.00 with discharge completed fifteen minutes later. With it being a Wednesday, she is not scheduled to sail on her mid-week sailing to Belfast until 15.00. This allows me sufficient time to witness a General Emergency Exercise on the craft, which I do as part of my monitoring procedures on all the vessels. The *SuperSeaCat Two* completes a text book turn-round in Dublin, arriving at 12.22 and off the berth three minutes ahead of schedule at 13.12.

Not only is reliability extremely important but also punctuality, and in addition to all the ships' crews we are fortunate to have the

The **Ben-my-Chree** has proved an extremely reliable ship for the Company and has done over 501,972 nautical miles since she entered service in 1996. (Miles Cowsill)

*The **Lady of Mann** leaves for Liverpool in the evening sun. Note the cars parked on her outer car decks, a sure sign of a full load at the end of the TT period.*
(Miles Cowsill)

*The Italian-built **SuperSeaCat Two** inaugurated the Liverpool-Dublin service in 1998. As from 2005 she will maintain fast ferry operations for the Company in place of*
***SeaCat Isle of Man**. (Miles Cowsill)*

The **Lady of Mann** (2) swings in the inner harbour of Douglas with the backdrop of the Central Promenade behind. (Miles Cowsill)

*The **Ben-my-Chree** arrives off the port of Heysham on her morning sailing from the Island. In 2004 Heysham port celebrated its 100th anniversary.* (Miles Cowsill)

co-operation and dedication of all the traffic and terminal staff ashore headed in Douglas by Sean Orton and Heysham, Liverpool, Dublin and Belfast by Alice Rice, Janice Farroll, Gerry O'Kelly and Diane Poole respectively. Evidence of such efficiency sees the *Ben-my-Chree* off the berth at Heysham on time at 14.15 and the *SeaCat Isle of Man*, now under the command of Captain Terry Moore on her north-about route to Belfast, is already at Clay Head by her scheduled departure time of 15.00, having departed impressively ahead of it at 14.47.

As the office working day draws to a close it is business as usual for the vessels, with them all completing their respective voyages on or ahead of schedule. The turn-round teams ashore and afloat once again gear up for crew changes, bunkering, stores replenishment and in general a seamless transition as far as our customers are concerned.

Although the office doors may close, the lines of communication remain firmly open with 24-hour access to all the Executive Directors and Senior Managers through various means.

Since the earlier part of the day the weather has improved with the wind veering to the west and moderating to just a moderate breeze. Consequently, the *SuperSeaCat Two*, under the command of Captain Ryan Kevan, arrives in Douglas just ahead of schedule and berths at No. 5 which has been vacated by the departure of the *Ben-my-Chree* at 19.39 under the skilful hand of Captain Roger Moore. By the time of the SuperSeaCat's arrival, the *SeaCat Isle of Man* has already discharged on No. 1 berth after her arrival from Belfast, and as her next sailing is not until the next morning some planned maintenance is undertaken under the watchful eye of the Duty Chief Engineer. He is ably assisted by our shore-based maintenance team headed by Charlie Coole.

The Company has always been renowned for the high standard of maintenance and operation of its vessels but of equal

importance is the competence of its officers and crews. Because of the different work patterns and schedules of the ships and less stringent regulations, it used to be possible for one crew to 'man' each vessel throughout the summer season. That has long since changed as evidenced in the number of crew changes mentioned previously.

In order for the vessels to be in compliance with the latest legislation, the Personnel Office, and Andrew Kennish in particular under the supervision of the Human Resources Director Stuart Garrett, ensure all the vessels are appropriately crewed at all times. Most training courses are also arranged through this department, and along with succession planning is an important facet now and for the future which the Board of Directors firmly embrace and to which they are fully committed, as a means of ensuring the high standards of which the Company is justifiably proud can be maintained.

As the sun sets on yet another waypoint day which is the history of the Steam Packet, the last sailing of the day is taken by the *SuperSeaCat* at 22.28, arriving back in Liverpool at 00.55. Meanwhile, the *Ben-my-Chree* has arrived in Heysham and is already loading all the essential commodities, which are the lifeblood at the heart of the Island's community. As Captain Moore safely manoeuvres her out of Heysham at 02.10, so another day in the long and magnificent history of the Company begins and the course is set fair for it to reach and pass well beyond this its 175th Anniversary.

Throughout my time in the Company there have been many changes and no doubt there will be many more to come, but I have always been immensely proud to serve in it and it has been a very great privilege to do so in my various capacities ashore and afloat.

*The **Manx Maid** (1) lying in the Mersey some time before the Second World War. On her return from service as an Armed Boarding Vessel, her mainmast, which had been removed, was never replaced. (John Clarkson collection)*

*The **Ramsey Town** was formerly the Midland Railway's **Antrim** of 1904 and is seen en route to Ardrossan. (Bruce Peter collection)*

*The **Fenella** (2) approaching Ardrossan and showing her distinctive black-painted bulwarks which was the only easy way of identifying the vessel from her virtually identical sister ship, **Tynwald** (4). (Bruce Peter collection)*

CHAPTER FOURTEEN

Fleet List 1840-2005
Compiled by John Shepherd

1 Mona's Isle [1] *Wooden paddle steamer, side lever*

Built: John Wood & Co, Port Glasgow Engines: Robert Napier, Glasgow
Gross Tonnage: 200 Speed: 8.5 knots
Overall length: 35.36m Breadth: 5.79m
Launched: 30.6.1830 Cost: £7,052
Disposal: Sold to Robert Napier for breaking up in 1851 for £580.

2 Mona [1] *Wooden paddle steamer, side lever*

Built: John Wood & Co, Port Glasgow Engines: Robert Napier, Glasgow
Gross Tonnage: 150 Speed: 9 knots
Overall length: 29.87m Breadth: 5.18m
Launched: 27.7.1832 Cost: £4,650
Disposal: Sold to Liverpool Steam Tug Co. in 1841.

3 Queen of the Isle *Wooden paddle steamer, side lever*

Built & engined: Robert Napier, Glasgow
Gross Tonnage: 350 Speed: 9.5 knots
Overall length: 39.01m Breadth: 6.55m
Launched: 3.5.1834
Disposal: Sold to Napier in 1844 and converted to sail. Wrecked off
        Falklands.

4 King Orry [1] *Wooden paddle steamer, side lever*

Official Number: 21923 Call Sign: N J H M
Built: John Winram, Douglas Engines: Robert Napier, Glasgow
Gross Tonnage: 433 Speed: 9.5 knots
Overall length: 42.67m Breadth: 7.09m
Launched: 10.2.1842 Cost: £10,763
Disposal: Taken over by Napier in 1858 in part payment for **Douglas** [1]
        (£5,000 allowed). Re-sold to Greeks by Napier for trading in
        Eastern Mediterranean.

5 Ben-My-Chree [1] *Iron paddle steamer, side lever*

Official Number: 21922 Call Sign: N J H L
Built & engined: Robert Napier, Glasgow (engines ex **Queen of the Isle**)
Yard No. 13
Gross Tonnage: 458 Speed: 9.5 knots
Overall length: 50.29m Breadth: 7.01m
Launched: 3.5.1845 Cost: £11,500
Disposal: Sold in 1860 for further trading in West Africa for £1,200.
        Reported to be lying as a hulk in the Bonny River in 1930.

6 Tynwald [1] *Iron paddle steamer, side lever*

Official Number: 21921 Call Sign: N J H K
Built & engined: Robert Napier, Glasgow
Yard No. 19
Gross Tonnage: 700 Speed: 14 knots
Overall length: 57.30m Breadth: 8.23m
Launched: 28.4.1846 Cost: £21,500
Disposal: Sold in 1866 for £5,000 to Caird & Co. in part payment for
        Tynwald [2].

7 Mona's Queen [1] *Iron paddle steamer, side lever*

Official Number: 21930 Call Sign: N J H N
Built: J & G Thomson, Govan
Yard No. 6
Gross Tonnage: 600 Speed: 13 knots
Overall length: 56.69m Breadth: 8.23m
Launched: 27.11.1852 Cost: £14,000
Disposal: Broken up in 1880.

8 Douglas [1] *Iron paddle steamer, side lever*

Official Number: 20683 Call Sign: N C F T
Built & engined: Robert Napier, Glasgow
Yard No. 87
Gross Tonnage: 700 Speed: 17 knots
Overall length: 62.48m Breadth: 7.92m
Launched: 28.4.1858 Cost: £22,500
Disposal: Sold in 1862 for £24,000 to the Confederate Agents, Fraser
        Trenholm & Co. and renamed **Margaret & Jessie** as blockade
        runner in American Civil War. Commissioned as the **USS
        Gettysburg** in 1864. Broken up 1879 at Naples.

9 Mona's Isle [2]/Ellan Vannin built as *Iron paddle steamer, simple
oscillating*

Official Number: 27260 Call Sign: P Q M G
Built & engined: Tod & McGregor, Meadowside, Glasgow
Converted to twin screw steamer in 1883 by Westray, Copeland & Co.,
Barrow and renamed **Ellan Vannin** on 16th November 1883. 2 cylinder
compound engines installed.
Gross Tonnage: 339/375 as E/V Speed: 12/12.5 knots as E/V
Overall length: 63.09m Breadth: 6.71m
Launched: 10.4.1860 Cost: £10,673
Disposal: Foundered at Mersey Bar at 07.00 on 3rd December 1909 with
        loss of all on board.

10 Snaefell [1] *Iron paddle steamer, 2 cylinder oscillating*

Official Number: 45468   Call Sign: V D L F
Built & engined: Caird & Co., Greenock
Yard No. 105
Gross Tonnage: 700   Speed: 15 knots
Overall length: 69.68m   Breadth: 8.00m
Launched: 22.6.1863   Cost: £22,000
Disposal: Sold in 1875 for £15,500 to Zeeland Steamship Co. and renamed **Stad Breda**. Broken up in 1888 at Ambacht, Holland.

11 Douglas [2] *Iron paddle steamer, 2 cylinder oscillating*

Official Number: 45470   Call Sign: V D L H
Built & engined: Caird & Co., Greenock
Yard No. 112
Gross Tonnage: 709   Speed: 15 knots
Overall length: 69.19m   Breadth: 7.98m
Launched: 11.5.1864   Cost: £24,869
Disposal: Auctioned in January 1889 by C. W. Kellock & Co. for £1,450 for scrapping by R. P. Houston.

12 Tynwald [2] *Iron paddle steamer, 2 cylinder oscillating*

Official Number: 45474   Call Sign: H P T J
Built & engined: Caird & Co., Greenock
Yard No. 131
Gross Tonnage: 696   Speed: 15 knots
Overall length: 73.53m   Breadth: 8.02m
Launched: 17.3.1866   Cost: £26,000
Disposal: Auctioned in January 1889 by C.W. Kellock & Co. for scrapping by George Cohen.

13 King Orry [2] *Iron paddle steamer, simple oscillating*

Official Number: 45479   Call Sign: P K G B
Built: R. Duncan & Co., Port Glasgow
Yard No. 56
Engines: Rankin & Blackmore, Greenock
Gross Tonnage: 809 inc. to 1104 Speed: 15 knots
Overall length: 79.25m (as built) Breadth: 8.94m
Launched: 27.3.1871   Cost: £26,000
Refitted by Westray, Copeland & Co., Barrow in 1888 and lengthened by 9.14m. New compound diagonal engines increased speed to 17 knots.
Disposal: Broken up at Llanerch-y-Mor, Deeside in 1912.

14 Ben-my-Chree [2] *Iron paddle steamer, 2 cylinder oscillating*

Official Number: 67288   Call Sign: P K F Q
Built & engined: Barrow Shipbuilding Co. Ltd
Yard No. 25
Refitted and reboilered 1884 - Two additional funnels fitted
Gross Tonnage: 1030 inc. to 1192 Speed: 14 knots
Overall length: 96.93m   Breadth: 9.45m
Launched: 6.5.1875   Cost: £38,000
Disposal: Broken up in 1906 at Morecambe by T. W. Ward & Co.

15 Snaefell [2] *Iron paddle steamer, simple oscillating*

Official Number: 67289   Call Sign: Q W S P
Built & engined: Caird & Co., Greenock
Yard No. 202
Gross Tonnage: 849   Speed: 15 knots
Overall length: 79.10m   Breadth: 8.91m
Launched: 27.4.1876   Cost: £28,250
Disposal: Towed to Holland by tug **Ostzee** for demolition in 1904.

16 Mona [2] *Iron single screw steamer, vertical compound engines*

Official Number: 76302
Built & engined: William Laird & Co., Birkenhead
Yard No. 56
Gross Tonnage: 562   Speed: 13 knots
Overall length: 63.09m   Breadth: 7.92m
Launched: 31.5.1878   Cost: £19,500
Disposal: Sank in the Formby Channel when she was run into by the Spanish steamer **Rita** on 5th August 1883.

17 Fenella [1] *Iron twin screw steamer, vertical compound engines*

Official Number: 76303   Call Sign: J C T G
Built & engined: Barrow Shipbuilding Co. Ltd.
Yard No. 95
Gross Tonnage: 564   Speed: 14 knots
Overall length: 63.09m   Breadth: 7.92m
Launched: 9.6.1881   Cost: £18,750
Disposal: Sold for £2,290 in 1929 and broken up by John Cashmore at Newport, Gwent.

18 Mona's Isle [3] *Steel paddle steamer, compound oscillating*

Official Number: 76304   Call Sign: P K F C
Built & engined: Caird & Co., Greenock
Yard No. 227
Gross Tonnage: 1564   Speed: 18 knots
Overall length: 103.02m Breadth: 11.58m
Launched: 16.5.1882   Cost: £58,700
Disposal: Purchased by Admiralty in 1915, and broken up by T. W. Ward Ltd at Morecambe in 1919.

19 Peveril [1] *Steel twin screw steamer, vertical compound engines*

Official Number: 76307   Call Sign: J R Q V
Built & engined: Barrow Shipbuilding Co. Ltd.
Yard No. 121
Gross Tonnage: 561   Speed: 13.5 knots
Overall length: 65.53m   Breadth: 7.92m
Launched: 24.5.1884   Cost: £20,000
Disposal: Sank off Douglas on 16th September 1899 after collision with **Monarch**.

*The **Tynwald** (4) under way in the Firth of Clyde, enabling a comparison to be made with her sister ship the **Fenella** (2) on page 142. (Bruce Peter collection)*

*A fine photograph of the **Ben-my-Chree** (4) shortly after being painted white in 1932 and showing the lines of this classic cross-Channel steamer to full advantage.*
(John Clarkson collection)

The **Lady of Mann** (1) was probably the best-loved of all Steam Packet vessels although her extra freeboard made her unpopular with many of the older Masters who preferred the 'kinder' but older **Ben-my-Chree** (4). (John Clarkson collection)

The **Mona's Queen** (3) at anchor in the Mersey showing her extra deck forward which caused problems for her Captains in certain weather conditions. (John Clarkson collection)

20 Mona's Queen [2] *Steel paddle steamer, compound oscillating*

Official Number: 76308   Call Sign: K F L S
Built & engined: Barrow Shipbuilding Co. Ltd.
Yard No. 130
Gross Tonnage: 1559   Speed: 19 knots
Overall length: 99.98m   Breadth: 11.66m
Launched: 18.4.1885   Cost: £55,000
Disposal: Sold in 1929 for £5,920 for breaking up by Smith & Houston
          at Port Glasgow.

21 Prince of Wales *Steel paddle steamer, compound diagonal*

Official Number: 93381   Call Sign: P K D B
Built & engined: Fairfield Shipbuilding & Engineering Co. Ltd., Govan
Yard No. 322
Built for IOM, Liverpool & Manchester S.S. Co. (Manx Line)
Acquired by IOMSPCo: 23.11.1888
Gross Tonnage: 1657   Speed: 20.25 knots
Overall length: 104.09m   Breadth: 11.89m
Launched: 14.4.1887   Cost (on acquisition): £77,500
Disposal: Sold to Admiralty in 1915 and name changed to **Prince
          Edward**. Sold to T.C.Pas for £5,600 in 1920 and broken up at
          Scheveningen, Holland.

22 Queen Victoria *Steel paddle steamer, compound diagonal*

Official Number: 93379   Call Sign: P K C S
Built & engined: Fairfield Shipbuilding & Engineering Co. Ltd. Govan
Yard No. 321
Built for IOM, Liverpool & Manchester S.S. Co. (Manx Line)
Acquired by IOMSPCo: 23.11.1888
Gross Tonnage: 1657   Speed: 20.25 knots
Overall length: 104.09m   Breadth: 11.89m
Launched: 29.3.1887   Cost: £77,500
Disposal: Sold to Admiralty 28.1.1915. Sold for breaking up at Ambacht,
          Holland for £5,450 in April 1920.

23 Tynwald [3] *Steel twin screw steamer, triple expansion*

Official Number: 95755   Call Sign: P K G D
Built & engined: Fairfield Shipbuilding & Engineering Co. Ltd., Govan
Yard No. 356
Gross Tonnage: 937   Speed: 18 knots
Overall length: 84.12m   Breadth: 10.36m
Launched: 11.5.1891   Cost: £58,683
Disposal: Laid up in 1930. Sold to R. A. Colby Cubbin in 1933 and
          renamed **Western Isles**. Req. by Admiralty in 1939 and
          renamed **Eastern Isles**. Broken up at La Spezia in 1952.

24 Empress Queen *Steel paddle steamer, compound diagonal*

Official Number: 95759   Call Sign: P V R M
Built & engined: Fairfield Shipbuilding & Engineering Co. Ltd., Govan
Yard No. 392
Gross Tonnage: 2140   Speed: 21.5 knots
Overall length: 113.39m   Breadth: 13.11m
Launched: 4.3.1897   Cost: £130,000
Disposal: Req. by Admiralty 1915. Stranded on Bembridge Ledge, Isle of
          Wight, 1.2.1916 and became total loss.

25 Douglas [3] *Steel single screw steamer, reciprocating engines*

Official Number: 94515   Call Sign: L C S W
Built & engined: Robert Napier, Glasgow.
Yard No. 416
Built as the **Dora** for the London & South Western Railway Co.
Acquired by the IOMSP Co: 26.7.1901
Gross Tonnage: 774   Speed: 15 knots
Overall length: 75.89m   Breadth: 9.14m
Launched: 2.3.1889   Cost (on acquisition): £13,500
Disposal: Sank in River Mersey after collison with **Artemisia** on
          16.8.1923.

26 Mona [3] *Steel paddle steamer, compound diagonal*

Official Number: 96575   Call Sign: L J R V
Built & engined: Fairfield Shipbuilding & Engineering Co. Ltd., Govan
Yard No. 340
Built as **Calais-Douvres** for London, Chatham & Dover Railway Co.
Sold in 1900 to Liverpool & Douglas Steamers
Acquired by IOMSPCo: July 1903
Gross Tonnage: 1212   Speed: 18 knots
Overall length: 102.41m   Breadth: 10.97m
Launched: 13.4.1889   Cost (on acquisition): £6,000
Disposal: Broken up at Briton Ferry by T. W. Ward Ltd. in 1909.

27 Viking *Steel triple screw direct drive turbine steamer*

Official Number: 118604   Call Sign: H R C S:
                                          from 1934 G P M D
Built: Armstrong, Whitworth, Newcastle on Tyne
Yard No. 719
Turbines: Parsons Marine Steam Turbine Co. Ltd.
Gross Tonnage: 1957   Speed: 22.5 knots
Overall length: 110.03m   Breadth: 12.80m
Launched: 7.3.1905   Cost : £83,900
Disposal: Sold to T. W. Ward Ltd. at Barrow for breaking up on
          16.8.1954.

28 Ben-my-Chree [3] *Steel triple screw direct drive turbine steamer*

Official Number: 118605   Call Sign: H R C Q
Built & engined: Vickers, Sons & Maxim, Barrow in Furness
Yard No. 365
Gross Tonnage: 2550   Speed: 24.5 knots
Overall length: 118.57m   Breadth: 14.02m
Launched: 24.3.1908   Cost: £112,100
Disposal: Sunk by gunfire at Castellorizo 11.1.1917. Raised 1920.
          Scrapped at Venice 1923.

29 Snaefell [3] *Steel twin screw steamer, triple expansion*

Official Number: 118606   Call Sign: H S B Q
Built & engined: Cammell Laird & Co. Ltd., Birkenhead
Yard No. 758
Gross Tonnage: 1368   Speed: 19 knots
Overall length: 85.95m   Breadth: 12.60m
Launched: 12.2.1910   Cost: £59,275
Disposal: Req. by Admiralty 1914. Torpedoed and sunk in Mediterranean
          5.6.1918.

30 Tyrconnel *Steel single screw steamer, compound engine*

Official Number: 99794	Call Sign: N D P B

Built & engined: J. Fullerton, Paisley
Yard No. 103
Acquired by Manx Steam Trading Co. in 1902
Acquired by IOMSP Co: 6.5.1911

Gross Tonnage: 274	Speed: 9 knots
Overall length: 41.15m	Breadth: 6.71m
Launched: 29.2.1892	Cost (on acquisition): £4,875

Disposal: Sold to W. J. Ireland of Liverpool January 1932. Broken up at Danzig 1934.

31 The Ramsey *Steel twin screw steamer, reciprocating*

Official Number: 104240	Call Sign: M N S P

Built & engined: The Naval Construction & Armaments Co., Barrow
Yard No. 243
Built as the ***Duke of Lancaster*** for the Lancashire & Yorkshire Railway Co.
Acquired by IOMSPCo.: 12.7.1912

Gross Tonnage: 1621	Speed: 17.5 knots
Overall length: 97.54m	Breadth: 11.28m
Launched: 9.5.1895	

Disposal: Requisitioned by Admiralty 1914. Sunk by German raider *Meteor* 8.8.1915.

32 Peel Castle *Steel twin screw steamer, reciprocating*

Official Number: 104233	Call Sign: J F K Q

Built & engined: William Denny & Bros., Dumbarton
Yard No. 480
Built as **Duke of York** for the Lancashire & Yorkshire Railway Co.
Acquired by IOMSPCo.: 17.7.1912

Gross Tonnage: 1474	Speed: 17.5 knots
Overall length: 97.84m	Breadth: 11.28m
Launched: 28.2.1894	

Disposal: Broken up by Arnott Young at Dalmuir, Clyde, February 1939.

33 King Orry [3] *Steel twin screw steamer, geared turbines*

Official Number: 118608	Call Sign: J F P C
	from 1934: G P M F

Built & engined: Cammell Laird & Co. Ltd., Birkenhead
Yard No. 789

Gross Tonnage: 1877	Speed: 20.75 knots
Overall length: 95.40m	Breadth: 13.11m
Launched: 11.3.1913	Cost: £96,000

Disposal: Bombed and sunk in the evacuation of Dunkirk 30.5.1940.

34 Mona [4] *Steel twin screw steamer, triple expansion.*

Official Number: 124188	Call Sign: H K T G
	from 1934: G F B Y

Built & engined: Fairfield Shipbuilding & Engineering Co. Ltd., Govan
Yard No. 451
Built as **Hazel** for the Laird Line
Acquired by IOMSPCo.: 21.5.1919

Gross Tonnage: 1219	Speed: 16 knots
Overall length: 81.69m	Breadth: 10.97m
Launched: 13.4.1907	Cost (on acquisition): £65,000

Disposal: Sold to E. G. Rees of Llanelli for breaking up, December 1938.

35 Manxman [1] *Steel triple screw steamer, direct drive turbines*

Official Number: 118603	Call Sign: H M R S
	from 1934: G F P S

Built & engined: Vickers, Sons & Maxim, Barrow
Yard No. 315
Built as **Manxman** for Midland Railway Co.
Acquired by IOMSPCo.: March 1920

Gross Tonnage: 2030	Speed: 22 knots
Overall length: 103.94m	Breadth: 13.11m
Launched: 15.6.1904	

Disposal: Requisitioned by Admiralty 1939. Broken up by T. W. Ward at Preston 1949.

36 Mona's Isle [4] *Steel triple screw steamer, direct drive turbines.*

Official Number: 120522	Call Sign: H C M F:
	from 1934: G F P M

Built & engined: William Denny & Bros., Dumbarton
Yard No. 751
Built as **Onward** for South Eastern & Chatham Railway Co.
Acquired by IOMSPCo.: May 1920.   Name changed: 27.8.1920

Gross Tonnage: 1691	Speed: 21 knots
Overall length: 96.93m	Breadth: 12.19m
Launched: 11.3.1905	

Disposal: Sold for breaking up in October 1948 and towed to Milford Haven.

37 Snaefell [4] *Steel triple screw steamer, direct drive turbines.*

Official Number: 121331	Call Sign: H G F M:
	from 1934: G P M K

Built & engined: Fairfield Shipbuilding & Engineering Co. Ltd., Govan
Yard No. 444
Built as **Viper** for .G. & J. Burns
Acquired by IOMSPCo.: 22.3.1920.   Name changed: 22.7.1920

Gross Tonnage: 1713	Speed: 21 knots
Overall length: 99.21m	Breadth: 12.04m
Launched: 10.3.1906	Cost (on acquisition): £60,000

Disposal: Sold to Smith & Houston, Port Glasgow 1945, scrapped 1948.

38 Cushag *Steel single screw steamer, compound engines*

Official Number: 124673	Call Sign: M D Y P

Built & engined: George Brown & Co., Greenock
Yard No. 50
Built as **Ardnagrena** for J. Waterson, Co. Antrim: sold in 1914 to Humber Steam Coasters.
Acquired by IOMSPCo.: May 1920.   Name changed: 27.8.1920.

Gross Tonnage: 223	Speed: 10 knots
Overall length: 39.62m	Breadth: 6.71m
Launched: 12.8.1908	Cost (on acquisition): £22,000

Disposal: Sold 26.1.1943 to T. Dougal and registered at Stornoway: broken up Grangemouth July 1957.

The **Snaefell (4)** was originally G&J Burns' **Viper** and carried this emblem on her stern throughout her Steam Packet career. Built at Fairfield's in 1906, she was acquired by the Steam Packet in 1920 and served until 1948. (John Clarkson collection)

The **Peel Castle** came to the Steam Packet in 1912 and was originally the Lancashire & Yorkshire Railway's **Duke of York**. She was broken up in 1939. (John Clarkson collection)

39 Manx Maid [1] *Steel triple screw steamer, direct drive turbines*

Official Number: 131763

Call Sign: H R Q M:
from 1934: G K M F

Built & engined: Cammell Laird & Co. Ltd., Birkenhead
Yard No. 761
Built as **Caesarea** for the London & South Western Railway Co.:
Acquired by IOMSPCo.: 27.11.1923.

Gross Tonnage: 1504

Speed: 20 knots

Overall length: 90.83m

Breadth: 11.89m

Launched: 26.5.1910

Cost: £38,500 (inc. complete refit)

Disposal: Broken up at Barrow in 1950 by T. W. Ward & Co. Ltd.

40 Ben-my-Chree [4] *Steel twin screw steamer, geared turbines*

Official Number: 145304

Call Sign: L C F G:
from 1934: G N D B

Built & engined: Cammell Laird & Co. Ltd., Birkenhead
Yard No. 926

Gross Tonnage: 2586

Speed: 22.5 knots

Overall length: 111.56m

Breadth: 14.02m

Launched: 5.4.1927

Cost: £200,000

Maiden Voyage: 29.6.1927

Final Voyage: 13.9.1965

Disposal: Left Birkenhead under tow of tug **Fairplay XI** on 18.12.1965 for shipbreakers at Ghent.

41 Victoria *Steel triple screw steamer, direct drive turbines*

Official Number: 123811

Call Sign: H K N R
from 1934: G N T F

Built & engined: William Denny & Bros., Dumbarton
Yard No. 789
Built as **Victoria** for South Eastern & Chatham Railway Co.
Acquired by IOMSPCo.: 1928

Gross Tonnage: 1641

Speed: 21 knots

Overall length: 98.15m

Breadth: 12.19m

Launched: 27.2.1907

Cost (on acquisition): £25,000

Disposal: Last voyage: 18.8.1956. Towed from Birkenhead to Barrow 25.1.1957 and broken up by T. W. Ward & Co. Ltd.

42 Ramsey Town *Steel twin screw steamer, triple expansion reciprocating*

Official Number: 116015

Call Sign: H M S B

Built & engined: John Brown & Co. Ltd., Clydebank
Yard No. 363
Built as **Antrim** for the Midland Railway Co.
Acquired by IOMSPCo.: 11.5.1928

Gross Tonnage: 1954

Speed: 20 knots

Overall length: 103.63m

Breadth: 12.80m

Launched: 22.4.1904

Cost (on acquisition): £14,612

Disposal: Broken up at Preston in October 1936 by T. W. Ward & Co. Ltd.

43 Rushen Castle *Steel twin screw steamer, triple expansion reciprocating*

Official Number: 109661

Call Sign: Q F W M
from 1934: G F R X

Built & engined: Vickers, Sons & Maxim Ltd., Barrow
Yard No. 264
Built as **Duke of Cornwall** for the Lancashire & Yorkshire and London & North Western Railway Companies' Joint Service
Acquired by IOMSPCo.: 11.5.1928

Gross Tonnage: 1724

Speed: 17.5 knots

Overall length: 97.84m

Breadth: 11.28m

Launched: 23.4.1898

Cost: (on acquisition) £29,254

Disposal: Last voyage: 14.9.1946. Towed from Douglas to Ghent on 9.1.1947 by tug **Ganges** for demolition.

44 Peveril [2] *Steel single screw steamer, triple expansion*

Official Number: 145306

Call Sign: M B F C

Built & engined: Cammell Laird & Co. Ltd., Birkenhead
Yard No. 957

Gross Tonnage: 798

Speed: 12 knots

Overall length: 64.92m

Breadth: 10.52m

Launched: 25.4.1929

Cost: £42,600

Disposal: Broken up at Glasson Dock, May 1964.

45 Lady of Mann [1] *Steel twin screw steamer, geared turbines*

Official Number: 145307

Call Sign: L G C Q
from 1934: G M K Z

Built & engined: Vickers Armstrong Ltd., Barrow
Yard No. 660

Gross Tonnage: 3104

Speed: 22.5 knots

Overall length: 113.08m

Breadth: 15.30m

Launched: 4.3.1930

Cost: £249,073

Maiden Voyage: 28.6.1930

Final Voyage: 17.8.1971

Disposal: Left Barrow 29.12.1971 under tow of tug **Wrestler**, for breaking up by Arnott Young, Dalmuir, arriving 31.12.1971.

46 Conister [1] *Steel single screw steamer, triple expansion reciprocating*

Official Number: 145470

Call Sign: K L F W
from 1934: M K W Q

Built & engined: Goole Shipbuilding Co. Ltd., Goole
Yard No. 4
Built as **Abington** for G. T. Gillie & Blair, Newcastle.
Acquired by IOMSPCo.: 8.1.1932

Gross Tonnage: 411

Speed: 10 knots

Overall length: 44.20m

Breadth: 7.31m

Launched: 13.9.1921

Cost (on acquisition): £5,500

Disposal: Left Douglas under tow of tug **Campaigner** for breaking up by Arnott Young, Dalmuir on 26.1.1965.

47 Mona's Queen [3] *Steel twin screw steamer, geared turbines*

Official Number: 145308

Call Sign: G W S G

Built & engined: Cammell Laird & Co. Ltd., Birkenhead
Yard No. 998

Gross Tonnage: 2756

Speed: 21.5 knots

Overall length: 106.68m

Breadth: 14.63m

Launched: 12.4.1934

Cost: £201,250

Disposal: Mined and sunk at Dunkirk 29.5.1940.

This atmospheric post-war view of the Edward Pier shows the **Viking** having just arrived from Fleetwood and unusually berthed stern-in. The cargo vessels **Peveril** (2) and **Conister** (1) are further up the harbour. (Henry Maxwell/ John Hendy collection)

The **Douglas** (3) was built as the **Dora** in 1889 for the London & South Western Railway. Purchased by the Steam Packet in 1901, she was sunk in the Mersey in 1923. (Manx Museum)

*The **Peveril** (2) at the Office Berth at Douglas opposite the Company's goods shed.* (Henry Maxwell/ John Hendy collection)

*The cargo vessel **Cushag** was built in 1908 and served the Steam Packet between 1920 and 1943.* (Stan Basnett collection)

48 Fenella [2] *Steel twin screw steamer, geared turbines*

Official Number: 145310   Call Sign: G Z N Y
Built & engined: Vickers Armstrong Ltd., Barrow
Yard No. 718
Gross Tonnage: 2376   Speed: 21 knots
Overall length: 95.86m   Breadth: 14.02m
Launched: 16.12.1936   Cost : £203,550
Disposal: Sunk by air attack at Dunkirk 29.5.1940.

49 Tynwald [4] *Steel twin screw steamer, geared turbines*

Official Number: 165281   Call Sign: G Z R L
Built & engined: Vickers Armstrong Ltd., Barrow
Yard No. 717
Gross Tonnage: 2376   Speed: 21.5 knots
Overall length: 95.86m   Breadth: 14.02m
Launched: 16.12.1936   Cost: £203,550
Disposal: Torpedoed and sunk at Bougie, Algeria, 12.11.1942.

50 King Orry [4] *Steel twin screw steamer, geared turbines*

Official Number: 165282   Call Sign: G M J M
Built & engined: Cammell Laird & Co. Ltd., Birkenhead
Yard No. 1169
Gross Tonnage: 2485   Speed: 21.5 knots
Overall length: 105.19m   Breadth: 14.38m
Launched: 22.11.1945   Cost: £402,095
Maiden Voyage: 18.1.1946   Final Voyage: 31.8.1975
Disposal: Towed to Glasson Dock by tug Sea Bristolian 5.11.1975.
    Towed to Kent (arrived 11.1.1978) and broken up at Strood,
    late 1979.

51 Mona's Queen [4] *Steel twin screw steamer, geared turbines*

Official Number: 165283   Call Sign: G M J R
Built & engined: Cammell Laird & Co. Ltd., Birkenhead
Yard No. 1170
Gross Tonnage: 2485   Speed: 21.5 knots
Overall length: 105.16m   Breadth: 14.38m
Launched: 5.2.1946   Cost: £411,241
Maiden Voyage: 26.6.1946   Final Voyage: 16.9.1961
Disposal: Left Barrow under own steam 12.11.1962 renamed **Barrow
    Queen** bound for Piraeus for further service as **Fiesta** for
    Chandris Lines. Broken up at Perama 9.1981.

52 Tynwald [5] *Steel twin screw steamer, geared turbines*

Official Number: 165284   Call Sign: G J V X
Built & engined: Cammell Laird & Co. Ltd., Birkenhead
Yard No. 1184
Gross Tonnage: 2487   Speed: 21.5 knots
Overall length: 105.12m   Breadth: 14.38m
Launched: 24.3.1947   Cost: £461,859
Maiden Voyage: 31.7.1947   Final Voyage: 26.8.1974
Disposal: Sold to John Cashmore Ltd., Newport, Gwent for breaking up
    in November 1974, but re-sold and towed to Spanish
    shipbreakers at Aviles by tug **Sea Bristolian** on 3.2.1975.

53 Snaefell [5] *Steel twin screw steamer, geared turbines*

Official Number: 165287   Call Sign: M A V K
Built & engined: Cammell Laird & Co. Ltd., Birkenhead
Yard No. 1192
Gross Tonnage: 2489   Speed: 21.5 knots
Overall length: 105.11m   Breadth: 14.38m
Launched: 11.3.1948   Cost: £504,448
Maiden Voyage: 24.7.1948   Final Voyage: 29.8.1977
Disposal: Sold to Rochdale Metal Recovery Company and towed by tug
    George V to Blyth, Northumberland on 24.8.1978. Arrived
    8.9.1978 and broken up by H. Kitson, Vickers & Co.

54 Mona's Isle [5] *Steel twin screw steamer, geared turbines*

Official Number: 165288   Call Sign: G C X Y
Built & engined: Cammell Laird & Co. Ltd., Birkenhead
Yard No. 1209
Gross Tonnage: 2491   Speed: 21.5 knots
Overall length: 105.16m   Breadth: 14.38m
Launched: 12.10.1950   Cost: £570,000
Maiden Voyage: 22.3.1951   Final Voyage: 27.8.1980
Disposal: Left Birkenhead under tow of tug **Afon Wen** on 30.10.1980 for
    Dutch shipbreakers Sloop-Berginsbedrijf van de Marec.

55 Fenella [3] *Steel single screw diesel motorship*

Official Number: 165289   Call Sign: M L F M
Built & engined: Ailsa Shipbuilding Co. Ltd., Troon
Yard No. 472
Gross Tonnage: 1019   Speed: 12.5 knots
Overall length: 64.01m   Breadth: 11.28m
Launched: 6.8.1951   Cost: £163,783
Disposal: Sold to Cypriot Juliet Shipping Co. and left Birkenhead on
    9.2.1973 as the **Vasso M** for further trading. Caught fire and
    sank in the Eastern Mediterranean, May 1978.

56 Manxman [2] *Steel twin screw steamer, geared turbines*

Official Number: 186349   Call Sign: M T Q C
Built & engined: Cammell Laird & Co. Ltd., Birkenhead
Yard No. 1259
Gross Tonnage: 2495   Speed: 21.5 knots
Overall length: 105.11m   Breadth: 15.24m
Launched: 8.2.1955   Cost: £847,000
Maiden Voyage: 21.5.1955   Final Voyage: 4.9.1982
Disposal: Sold to Marda (Squash) Ltd. and sailed under own steam to
    Preston Dock on 3.10.1982 carrying 1,000 passengers. Left
    Preston under tow of **Afon Las** on 5.11.1990, arriving
    Liverpool 6.11.1990. Left Liverpool 16.4.1994 under tow of
    Freebooter bound for Hull for use as nightclub. Moved to
    Pallion Yard, Sunderland, where she arrived on 12.09.97 under
    tow of tug **T.H. Dev**: for possible purchase by the Manxman
    Steamship Society, May 2002.

The **Tyrconnel** of 1892 was another astute purchase. She served the Company well during her 21-year Manx career. (Stan Basnett collection)

Built in 1955, the **Conister** (2) came third-hand to the Steam Packet in 1973 having previously served as the **Brentfield** and **Spaniel.** She was sold again in 1981. (Stan Basnett)

Seen arriving at Douglas, the **Peveril** *(3) was built at Troon in 1963 and converted into a container vessel during 1972. (Stan Basnett)*

The **Peveril** *(4) was the Steam Packet's first roll on – roll off vessel. Built in Finland in 1971, the ship came to the Steam Packet on charter ten years later as the* **NF Jaguar**. *The following year she was renamed* **Peveril** *(4) and lasted until 1998. (Miles Cowsill)*

*Dressed overall at Fleetwood, the **Lady of Mann** (2) makes an impressive sight prior to a special sailing to Douglas.* (Captain Vernon Kinley)

*The **Tynwald** (6) outward bound from Douglas during her first season on the Heysham service.* (IOMSP Co Ltd)

57 Manx Maid [2] *Steel twin screw steamer, geared turbines*

Official Number: 186352	Call Sign: G H X Y
Built & engined: Cammell Laird & Co. Ltd., Birkenhead	
Yard No. 1303	
Gross Tonnage: 2724	Speed: 21.5 knots
Overall length: 104.83m	Breadth: 16.16m
Launched: 23.1.1962	Cost: £1,087,000
Maiden Voyage: 23.5.1962	Final Voyage: 9.9.1984

Disposal: Left Birkenhead under tow for Bristol 10.4.1985. Left Avonmouth 8.2.1986 under tow of tug **Indomitable** for Garston, Merseyside, for breaking up.

58 Peveril [3] *Steel single screw diesel motorship*

Official Number: 186353	Call Sign: G M O G
Built & engined: Ailsa Shipbuilding Co. Ltd., Troon	
Yard No. 516	

Converted to a Cellular Container Ship 1972 - Capacity 56 TEU

Gross Tonnage: 1048	Speed: 12 knots
Overall length: 62.48m	Breadth: 11.89m
Launched: 6.12.1963	Cost: £279,921

Disposal: Final Voyage 19.6.1981. Sold for further trading as **Nadalena H.**

59 Ramsey *Steel single screw diesel motorship*

Official Number: 186354	Call Sign: G P J H
Built & engined: Ailsa Shipbuilding Co. Ltd., Troon	
Yard No. 519	
Gross Tonnage: 446	Speed: 10 knots
Overall length: 45.42m	Breadth: 8.53m
Launched: 6.11.1964	Cost: £158,647

Disposal: Sold to R. Lapthorn & Co. of Rochester for further trading and renamed **Hoofort**. Left Birkenhead 9.1.1974. Re-sold in 1982 for further trading in the Cape Verde Islands and renamed **Boa Entrado**.

60 Ben-my-Chree [5] *Steel twin screw steamer, geared turbines*

Official Number: 186355	Call Sign: G R X Y
Built & engined: Cammell Laird & Co. Ltd., Birkenhead	
Yard No. 1320	
Gross Tonnage: 2762	Speed: 21.5 knots
Overall length: 104.83m	Breadth: 16.13m
Launched: 10.12.1965	Cost: £1,400,000
Maiden Voyage: 12.5.1966	Final Voyage: 19.9.1984

Disposal: Sold to New England Development Co. of Cincinnati for use as restaurant ship at Jacksonville, Florida, USA. Chartered back to IOMSPCo. from 25.5.1985 until 10.6.1985. Re-sold to shipbreakers at Santander, Spain. Left Birkenhead under tow of tug **Hollygarth** on 16.8.1989.

61 Mona's Queen [5] *Steel twin screw 10 Cyl. Pielstick diesel motorship*

Official Number: 307621	Call Sign: G P O W
Built & engined: Ailsa Shipbuilding Co. Ltd., Troon	
Yard No. 533	
Gross Tonnage: 2998	Speed: 21 knots
Overall length: 104.45m	Breadth: 16.74m
Launched: 22.12.1972	Cost: £2,100,000

Disposal: Final voyage 3.9.1990. Laid up Vittoria Dock, Birkenhead. Sold to MBRS Line, Philippines, November 1995. Renamed **Mary the Queen**. Left Birkenhead for Manila 4.12.1995.

62 Conister [2] *Steel single screw Sulzer motorship*

Official Number: 187114	Call Sign: G T V B
Built: George Brown & Co. Ltd., Greenock	
Yard No. 262	

Built in 1955 as **Brentfield** for Zillah Shipping Co. In 1959 became **Spaniel** of Coast Lines Group.
Acquired by IOMSPCo.: November 1973 (on charter July/November 1973)

Gross Tonnage: 891	Speed: 11 knots
Overall length: 68.28m	Breadth: 11.58m
Capacity: 46 TEU	Cost (on acquisition): £96,711

Disposal: Final voyage: 16.6.1981. Sold for breaking up at Aviles, Spain in November 1981.

63 Lady of Mann [2] *Steel twin screw 12 Cyl. Pielstick diesel motorship*

Official Number: 359761	Call Sign: G V E Q
Built : Ailsa Shipbuilding Co. Ltd., Troon	
Yard No. 547	
Gross Tonnage: 2990 (inc to 3083 in 1989)	Speed: 22 knots
Overall length: 104.43m	Breadth: 16.74m
Launched: 4.12.1975	Cost: £3,800,000

Still in service.

64 Peveril [4] *Steel twin screw Pielstick diesel motorship*

Official Number: 362507	Call Sign: G U Q N
Built: Kristiansands Mek Ver A/S, Norway	
Yard No. 216	

Built 1971 as **Holmia** for Silja Line; in 1973 became **ASD Meteor** of International Ship Chartering of Singapore and chartered to Sealink and renamed **Penda** until 1980. Name changed to **NF Jaguar** in P&O Group, Normandy Ferries. In 1981 **NF Jaguar** bareboat chartered by IOMSPCo. In November 1982 James Fisher of Barrow purchased **NF Jaguar** and chartered her to IOMSPCo. on long-term bareboat basis on agreed demise charter terms over 10 years. Name changed to **Peveril [4]**. Purchased outright by IOMSPCo. with a 'one-off' payment to James Fisher, May 1993.

Gross Tonnage: 1975	Speed: 14 knots
Overall length: 106.28m	Breadth: 16.03m

Disposal: Last voyage 6.7.1998. Laid up at Birkenhead. Sold to Marine Express Inc. of Puerto Rico August 2000. Renamed **Caribbean Express**. Sailed from Birkenhead 27.9.2000.

65 Mona's Isle [6] *Steel twin screw M.A.N. diesel motorship*

Official Number: 307718   Call Sign: G S N A
Built: NV Werf Gusto, Schiedam, Holland
Built as **Free Enterprise III** for Townsend Car Ferries, from 1968 Townsend-Thoresen. Sold to Mira Shipping Line in July 1984 and renamed **Tamira**.
Acquired by IOMSPCo. 26.10.1984 at Valletta, Malta and renamed **Mona's Isle**.
Gross Tonnage: 4657   Speed: 21 knots, maximum
Overall length: 117.51m   Breadth: 19.08m
Launched: 14.5.1966
Maiden Voyage for IOMSPCo.: 5.4.1985   Final Voyage: 5.10.1985
Disposal: Sold to Saudi Arabian owners for £710,500 and renamed **Al Fahad**. Left Birkenhead 7.4.1986 for further service in Red Sea.

66 Manx Viking *Steel twin screw Pielstick diesel motorship*

Official Number: 359765   Call Sign: G Z I A
Built: S A Juliana Const. Gijonesa, Gijon, Spain
Yard No. 243
Built as **Monte Castillo** for Naveria Aznar, Bilbao, Spain in 1976. Sold to Manx Line and renamed **Manx Viking** in March 1978. (Sealink/Manx Line from 20.10.1978). Manx Line merged with IOMSPCo. 1.4.1985 and **Manx Viking** taken on bareboat charter @ £1,500/day winter, £2,500/day summer.
Gross Tonnage: 3589   Speed: 17 knots
Overall length: 100.50m   Breadth: 16.76m
Disposal: Final voyage: 29.9.1986. Sold to Norwegian owners in February 1987 and renamed **Skudenes**. In April 1989 re-sold for service on the Canadian Great Lakes and renamed **Nindawayma** on the Tobermory/South Baymouth route across Georgian Bay.

67 Tynwald [6] *Steel twin screw Pielstick diesel motorship*

Official Number: 168903   Call Sign: G X S U
Built: Hawthorn Leslie (SB) Ltd., Hebburn on Tyne
Yard No. 765
Built as **Antrim Princess** for Caledonian Steam Packet (Irish Services) Ltd. Chartered to IOMSPCo. from 5.10.1985, first voyage 6.10.1985.
Gross Tonnage: 3762   Speed: 19.5 knots
Overall length: 112.63m   Breadth: 17.40m
Launched: 24.4.1967
Disposal: Final voyage: 19.2.1990. Laid up River Fal. Sold to Agostino Lauro of Naples and renamed **Lauro Express**. Left Falmouth 25.5.1990.

68 King Orry [5] *Steel twin screw Pielstick diesel motorship*

Call Sign: F N K C
Built: Cantieri Navali di Pietra Ligure, Italy
Yard No. 12
Built as **Saint Eloi**, renamed **Channel Entente** in May 1989.
Gross Tonnage: 4649   Speed: 19 knots
Overall length: 114.59m   Breadth: 18.62m
Launched: 26.2.1972   Cost [on acquisition]: £4.15million
Acquired by IOMSPCo.: 14.2.1990
First voyage 19.2.1990 as **Channel Entente**.
Renamed **King Orry** 8.12.1990.
Disposal: Final voyage 29.9.1998. Sold to Fion s.p.a. and renamed **Moby Love**. Left Birkenhead for Naples 23.10.1998.

69 Belard *Steel single screw MaK diesel motorship*

Official Number: 706568   Call Sign: G F M U
Built: 1979 by Frederikshavn Vaerft A/S, Frederikshavn, Denmark
Yard No. 380
Gross Tonnage: 1599   Speed: 15 knots
Overall length: 105.62m   Breadth: 18.83m
Capacity: 54 trailers
Chartered by Mannin Line from Pandoro Ltd.: first voyage 23.11.1993. Purchased from Pandoro Ltd.: 15.8.1994. Cost £3.2million. Chartered to IOMSP Co Ltd in 2002. Sold by the IOMSP Co in 1998. Now operates as the **Muirneag** for Caledonian MacBrayne between Ullapool and Stornoway.

70 SeaCat Isle of Man *Aluminium hulled fast craft catamaran*

Built: International Catamarans Pty. Ltd., Hobart, Tasmania
Call Sign: M W K D 7
Built 1991 as **Hoverspeed France**, chartered to Mediterranean operators as **Sardegna Express**: returned to UK and renamed **SeaCat Boulogne**.
Propulsion: 4 x 16 cylinder medium speed Ruston 16RK 270 marine diesel engines linked directly to 4 x Riva Lips BV waterjets.
Overall length: 73.6m   Breadth: 26.3m
Displacement tonnage: approx. 700 tonnes unloaded.
Speed: 37 knots (cruising), 42 knots maximum.
On charter to IOMSPCo. from Sea Containers from 20.6.1994.
First voyage: Douglas to Fleetwood 28.6.1994. Last Sailing: 20.10.04.

71 Ben-my-Chree [6] *Roll On/Roll Off Passenger Ferry*

Call Sign: M X L G 6
Built: 1998 by Van der Giessen-de Noord, Rotterdam
Yard No. 971
Launched: 4.4.1998   Cost: £24,000,000
Overall length: 124.90m   Breadth (moulded): 23.40m
Deadweight at design draft: 4,130 tons.
Gross Tonnage: 12,504   Service Speed: 19 knots
Passengers: 500   Total Trailer Lane Length: 1,235m
Maiden passenger carrying voyage: 4.8.1998.
Still in service.

OTHER VESSELS RECENTLY CHARTERED OR OPERATED BY THE COMPANY

1998-1999	**Claymore**
2000	**Dart I**
2002	**European Mariner**
2004	**Hoburgen**
2001-2004	**Rapide**
2002/2003	**Riverdance**
1998	**SeaCat Danmark**
1998, 2000, 2003-2005	**SuperSeaCat Two**
2000/2002	**SuperSeaCat Three**

the index

175